PREVENTION MAGAZINE'S
QUICK & HEALTHY LOW-FAT COOKING

Pastas and Sauces

Easy low-fat dishes based on one of the world's most versatile ingredients

✿ ✿ ✿

Rodale Press, Inc.
Emmaus, Pennsylvania

QUICK AND HEALTHY LOW-FAT COOKING

Managing Editor: JEAN ROGERS
Executive Editor: DEBORA A. TKAC
Senior Book Designer: ELIZABETH OTWELL
Art Director: JANE COLBY KNUTILA
Associate Art Director: FAITH HAGUE

Pastas and Sauces was produced by Rebus, Inc.
Recipe Development: MIRIAM RUBIN
Writer and Recipe Editor: BONNIE J. SLOTNICK
Art Director and Designer: JUDITH HENRY
Production Editor: SUE PAIGE

Photographer: ERIC JACOBSON
Nutritional analyses: HILL NUTRITION ASSOCIATES

Copyright © 1995 by Rodale Press, Inc.
Photographs copyright © 1995 by Eric Jacobson
Front Cover: Pasta Caesar Salad with Chicken (recipe on page 46)

All rights reserved. No part of this publication may be reproduced or transmitted in any form by any means, electronic or mechanical, including photocopying, recording or any other information storage and retrieval system, without the written permission of the publisher.

Prevention is a registered trademark of Rodale Press, Inc.

Printed in the United States of America on acid-free ∞, recycled paper, containing 15% post-consumer waste ♻

Library of Congress Cataloging-in-Publication Data

Pastas and sauces: Easy low-fat dishes based on one of the
    world's most versatile ingredients.
        p.   cm. — (quick & healthy low-fat cooking)
    "Managing editor Jean Rogers" — T.p. verso.
    Includes index.
    ISBN 0–87596–275–0   hardcover
    ISBN 0–87596–236–X   paperback
    1. Cookery (Pasta).   2. Sauces.   3. Quick and easy cookery.
4. Low-fat diet—Recipes   I. Rogers, Jean [date]. II. Prevention
(Emmaus, Pa.)   III. Series.
TX809.M17P373 1995
641.8'22—dc20   94–23900
                                                          CIP

Distributed in the book trade by St. Martin's Press

        4   6   8   10   9   7   5   3   hardcover
        4   6   8   10   9   7   5   3   paperback

CONTENTS

❧ ❧ ❧

Pasta with Poultry   *18*

Quick-cooking chicken and turkey turn pasta into
hearty dinners, satisfying salads and more

Pasta with Meat   *50*

Old and new favorites—from chunky sauce to satisfying
salad—made with the leanest cuts of beef, veal, pork and lamb

Pasta with Vegetables   *72*

The best of the garden's seasonal bounty, partnered
with pasta, makes quick colorful meals

Pasta with Seafood   *104*

A tempting variety, from a comforting salmon-noodle
casserole to an elegant scallop sauté

PREFACE

Our aim in creating this book was to give you recipes for dishes that are simple to prepare, that won't overextend your budget, that are deliciously healthy and that your family will love. We chose pasta as the topic because it's one food that's a favorite with everyone. You can dress it up for elegant dinner parties or make it casual for simple weekday suppers. And pasta will please even the most finicky eaters.

Pasta's only drawback is not so much a character flaw of its own as guilt by association: Pairing it with high-fat sauces undercuts its natural benefits. Keeping this in mind, we've taken extra care to come up with delicious, low-fat pasta dishes. The recipes we created were scrupulously tested, retested and taste-tested by demanding critics. It wasn't enough that the food met our strict dietary guidelines for fat, calories, cholesterol and sodium: If it didn't taste great, we sent it back to the kitchen.

Once we had the recipes worked out to our satisfaction, we pondered the best way to convince you of their palatability. It's not an original thought, but the old chestnut about a picture being worth a thousand words seemed to apply here. We know that when many people pick up a new cookbook, the recipes they're most tempted to try are the ones accompanied by photographs. So we decided to show you just how every recipe will turn out. With a full-page picture facing each recipe, you get a true idea of the finished dish. No surprises, no disappointments.

So you know at the outset how much time to budget for dinner preparation, we guide you with realistic cooking times. And we include other information you've told us in the past that you want, such as nutrient data, kitchen tips, step-by-step photos and more. All you have to do is follow the easy directions and dig into the luscious entrées you create in no time flat.

Jean Rogers

JEAN ROGERS
Food Editor
Prevention Magazine Health Books

INTRODUCTION

❧ ❧ ❧

Pasta is the perfect food for today's busy, health-conscious families. It cooks in a matter of minutes, comes in hundreds of shapes and lends itself to nearly endless combinations with other ingredients. It is an excellent source of complex carbohydrates, which are the best fuel for the body and the foundation of a healthy diet. Pasta is low in calories and fat, with about 200 calories and 1 gram of fat in a serving (2 ounces of uncooked pasta). Although egg noodles, fresh pasta and some brands of dried fettuccine contain eggs—and thus some cholesterol (about 55 milligrams per serving)—other dried pastas are cholesterol-free.

The fact is that the only way to turn pasta into a high-fat, high-calorie dish is to bury it under the wrong kind of sauce. The recipes and tips you'll find in this book will enable you to serve a tempting variety of satisfying pasta dishes that also boast exemplary nutritional profiles.

Today's supermarket shelves reflect the ever-growing popularity of pasta: Once simply stocked with spaghetti, elbow macaroni and egg noodles, they are now filled with the likes of savory cheese tortellini, hearty whole-wheat pappardelle and ruffled tricolor radiatore. On pages 14 through 17, you'll find an illustrated glossary of pastas, both old favorites and shapes you may not yet have enjoyed. Dry pasta keeps almost indefinitely if stored in a closed container in a cool place, and fresh pasta can be refrigerated for up to five days or frozen for about four months—so you can always have an assortment of pasta shapes on hand to give a new twist to a favorite dish.

There are some commonsense traditions about combining pastas with sauce: Pasta strands are generally served with smooth sauces, tubes and twists with chunky sauces, tiny pasta shapes in broth. But in the end, it's a matter of taste—of pleasing

the eye as well as the palate. So, although purists may frown, you can enjoy big, chewy rigatoni with pesto, or fragile angel-hair pasta with a chunky meat sauce. If the children in the family get a kick out of eating alphabets, stars, shells or cartwheels, go ahead and substitute these shapes for more pedestrian pastas.

On the next six pages you'll find a "pantry" of sauces to make in large quantities and freeze. Package the sauce in the amounts you need for family meals or freeze it in single-serving portions (each serving is enough to sauce 2 ounces of pasta, cooked). The recipes are accompanied by suggestions for variations, appropriate pastas and other ways to use the sauce. This section also includes a recipe for an Italian seasoning mix to use in the recipes in this book or in dishes of your own devising.

There's no secret to cooking perfect pasta, but here are a few tips to bring you great results every time. First, choose a good-quality pasta. Imported or domestic, it should be made from semolina flour, ground from durum wheat. Semolina pasta holds its shape and is less likely to turn mushy. Cook pasta in plenty of rapidly boiling water—about 4 quarts per pound of pasta—and stir the pasta as you add it to keep it from sticking together. The boiling will slow or stop as you add the pasta, but covering the pot will speed the water's return to a rolling boil. A range of cooking times is usually indicated on the package; to avoid overcooking, which destroys the pasta's texture, start checking for doneness after the shorter cooking time—or as soon as you suspect the pasta might be done. Take a bite of a piece of pasta: It should be firm but should not have a hard white core. Drain the pasta in a colander (rinse pasta only if you intend to use it in a salad), then transfer it to a warmed serving bowl. Mix in the sauce or other ingredients and, to enjoy the pasta at its best, serve it right away.

Spicy Marinara Sauce

❧ ❧ ❧

3 ounces sun-dried tomatoes (not packed in oil)

2 cups water

4 cans (28 ounces each) tomatoes in juice, drained

¼ cup extra-virgin olive oil

4 large onions, chopped

10 cloves garlic, minced

1 to 3 diced fresh jalapeño peppers (partially seeded or not, depending on desired hotness)

2 teaspoons dried basil, crumbled

1¼ teaspoons dried thyme, crumbled

1½ to 2 teaspoons crushed red pepper flakes

¾ teaspoon freshly ground pepper

3 bay leaves, preferably imported

½ teaspoon salt

¼ cup plus 2 tablespoons no-salt-added tomato paste

1 Place the dried tomatoes and water in a medium saucepan, cover and bring to a boil over high heat; remove the pan from the heat and let stand for 10 minutes. Drain and cool the tomatoes, then, using a sharp knife or kitchen shears, cut the tomatoes into small pieces.

2 Working in batches, process the drained canned tomatoes in a food processor until coarsely chopped.

3 In a Dutch oven or a large, heavy pot, heat the oil over high heat. Add the onions, garlic, jalapeño peppers, basil, thyme, red pepper flakes, black pepper, bay leaves and salt. Sauté for 2 minutes, then reduce the heat to medium-low, cover and cook, stirring frequently, for 15 minutes, or until the vegetables are very tender.

4 Add the sun-dried tomatoes, the chopped canned tomatoes and tomato paste, and stir well. Increase the heat to high and bring to a boil, then reduce the heat to medium-low, cover and simmer, stirring occasionally, for 30 minutes.

5 Uncover the sauce and simmer for 15 minutes longer, or until the sauce is thickened. Remove and discard the bay leaves.

Per serving 60 calories, 2 g. fat, 0.3 g. saturated fat, 0 mg. cholesterol, 203 mg. sodium **Serves 32 (makes 16 cups)**

PASTA CHOICES
penne, spaghetti, fusilli, orechietti

VARIATIONS
Salsa Puttanesca: Add ripe olives and drained canned tuna to Spicy Marinara Sauce.

Tomato Primavera: Add steamed vegetables, such as sliced zucchini or yellow squash, asparagus, green beans or broccoli florets, and sprinkle with grated Parmesan or Romano cheese.

Shrimp Marinara: Add shelled shrimp to the sauce and simmer just until the shrimp are done; serve over spinach fettuccine.

Marinara with Sausage: For 4 servings, brown 6 ounces of Italian turkey sausage. Add the sausage to 4 cups of Spicy Marinara Sauce and simmer until done.

OTHER USES
Dilute the sauce with broth and use it as a soup base, adding fresh or leftover vegetables and pasta or rice. Serve the sauce over baked fish or chicken.

TIPS
Freeze Spicy Marinara Sauce in ½-cup portions and use it in any recipe calling for tomato sauce.

Mushroom-Garlic Sauce

❧ ❧ ❧

1 large head garlic (about 3 ounces)

2 tablespoons olive oil

1 ounce dried mushrooms (about ½ cup)

2 cups boiling water

1 cup minced shallots

¾ teaspoon dried thyme, crumbled

¾ teaspoon salt

½ teaspoon freshly ground black pepper

¼ teaspoon dried sage

1½ pounds fresh white mushrooms, coarsely chopped

8 ounces fresh shiitake mushrooms, stems removed, caps coarsely chopped

2½ cups defatted reduced-sodium chicken broth

3 tablespoons cornstarch stirred into 3 tablespoons dry white wine or water

1 Preheat the oven to 375°. Rinse the garlic and place it on a square of foil; drizzle ½ teaspoon of oil over it. Wrap the garlic in the foil, place in a small pan and bake for 50 to 60 minutes, or until the garlic is very soft. Unwrap the garlic and let stand until cool enough to handle. Pinch or snip off the base of each clove and squeeze the pulp into a small bowl; mash the garlic with a fork and set aside.

2 Place the dried mushrooms in a heatproof bowl and pour the boiling water over them; let stand for 10 minutes, or until softened. Lift the mushrooms out of the water and transfer them to a large glass measuring cup. Suspend a cheesecloth-lined strainer over the measuring cup and strain the soaking liquid through it; set aside.

3 In a Dutch oven or large, heavy saucepan, heat the remaining 1 tablespoon plus 2½ teaspoons oil over medium-high heat. Stir in the shallots, thyme, salt, pepper and sage, and cook, stirring, for 3 to 4 minutes, or until the shallots are tender.

4 Stir in the the white mushrooms and shiitake mushrooms, and sauté, stirring often, for 5 to 6 minutes, or until the mushrooms release their juices and cook down to about half their volume.

5 Stir in the dried mushrooms with their soaking liquid, the mashed garlic and the broth; increase the heat to high and bring to a boil, stirring frequently. Reduce the heat to medium-low and simmer, stirring frequently, for 30 minutes to blend the flavors.

6 Stir in the cornstarch mixture; return the sauce to a boil, stirring, then simmer for 5 minutes longer.

Per serving 58 calories, 2 g. fat, 0.2 g. saturated fat, 0 mg. cholesterol, 208 mg. sodium **Serves 16 (makes 8 cups)**

PASTA CHOICES
spaghettini, fusilli, fettuccine, shells, penne, cavatappi, ridged macaroni

VARIATION
Tarragon Mushroom Sauce: Add 2 tablespoons coarsely chopped fresh tarragon to 2 cups of hot Mushroom-Garlic Sauce; toss with hot pasta. Sprinkle with 2 ounces of mild goat cheese.

OTHER USES
Serve Mushroom-Garlic Sauce over mashed or baked potatoes or other cooked vegetables.

TIPS
If fresh shiitake mushrooms are not available, use additional white mushrooms.
The sauce can be frozen for up to 2 months. If it seems thin when reheated, thicken it with cornstarch: To 2 cups of sauce add 1 tablespoon cornstarch mixed with 1 tablespoon water. Bring to a simmer and cook for a few minutes.

Slim Pesto

❦ ❦ ❦

8 cups loosely packed fresh basil leaves (about 3 large bunches)

1 cup defatted chicken or vegetable broth

3 tablespoons extra-virgin olive oil

2 tablespoons fresh lemon juice

1 teaspoon freshly ground pepper

1 teaspoon salt

5 garlic cloves, peeled

4 ounces freshly grated Parmesan or Romano cheese (to be added at serving time)

1 Wash and dry the basil leaves.

2 Combine half of the basil, ½ cup of the chicken broth, 1½ tablespoons of the oil, 1 tablespoon of the lemon juice, ½ teaspoon of the pepper and ½ teaspoon of the salt in a food processor. With the machine running, drop 3 garlic cloves through the feed tube and process until puréed. Scrape the mixture into a medium bowl.

3 Repeat with the remaining basil, broth, oil, lemon juice, pepper, salt and garlic cloves. Combine this with the first batch of pesto and mix well.

4 Divide the pesto among 4 small freezer containers or zip-closure freezer bags (each portion will be roughly a heaping half-cup, which will make 4 servings). Label and freeze for up to 2 months.

5 To serve, thaw the pesto completely, then add 1 ounce of the grated cheese to each portion and mix well. If the pesto seems very thick, add a little pasta cooking water when you drain the pasta.

Per serving 82 calories, 5 g. fat, 1.5 g. saturated fat, 5 mg. cholesterol, 317 mg. sodium **Serves 16 (makes 2⅓ cups)**

PASTA CHOICES

capellini, spaghettini or fettuccine; small filled pastas such as tortellini

VARIATIONS

Pesto Salad Dressing: Thin Slim Pesto with yogurt and use it as a dressing for pasta salads.

Chèvre Pesto: Substitute 1 ounce of mild goat cheese for the Parmesan.

Basil Marinara: Stir some Slim Pesto into Spicy Marinara Sauce (see page 8); add small cubes of fresh mozzarella and toss with hot pasta.

Fresh Tomato-Pesto Sauce: Combine the pesto with chopped ripe tomatoes and sliced Spanish onion.

OTHER USES

Stir Slim Pesto into puréed ricotta or cottage cheese for a creamy dip to serve with raw vegetables.

Serve Slim Pesto with minestrone or bean soup.

Add grated lemon zest and rub this "citrus pesto" over chicken or fish before grilling.

Mix 2 tablespoons of Slim Pesto with ⅓ cup light mayonnaise or low-fat sour cream to use as a sauce for cold fish or chicken, or for making tuna salad.

Stir Slim Pesto into cooked rice.

TIPS

The basil should be very fresh and the leaves unblemished. The best way to wash and dry a large quantity of herbs is in a salad spinner.

Thaw Slim Pesto in the refrigerator overnight, or thaw it briefly in a microwave (you don't want to cook it).

To thin the pesto a bit, making it easier to mix with the pasta, stir a tablespoon or so of the hot pasta cooking water into the pesto before adding it to the pasta.

Neo-Classic Bolognese Sauce

🌿 🌿 🌿

3 cans (28 ounces each) tomatoes in juice

2 pounds boneless skinless turkey breast, cut into chunks

5 tablespoons olive oil

3 large onions, chopped

2 green bell peppers, diced

8 garlic cloves, minced

1 tablespoon dried basil, crumbled

2 teaspoons dried oregano, crumbled

3 bay leaves, preferably imported

1 tablespoon granulated sugar

1½ teaspoons salt

1½ teaspoons freshly ground pepper

½ cup dry red wine, beef broth or chicken broth

2 cans (6 ounces each) no-salt-added tomato paste

1 One can at a time, process the canned tomatoes with their juice in a food processor; set aside.

2 In 2 or 3 batches, process the turkey in the food processor until finely ground.

3 In a large Dutch oven or large heavy pot, warm 2 tablespoons of the oil over high heat. Crumble in the turkey and cook, stirring occasionally, for 5 to 7 minutes, or until the turkey turns white. Transfer the cooked turkey to a bowl.

4 Warm the remaining 3 tablespoons oil in the pot over high heat. Stir in the onions, bell peppers, garlic, basil, oregano, bay leaves, sugar, salt and pepper. Reduce the heat to medium and cook the vegetables, stirring frequently, for 5 to 8 minutes, or until the onions and peppers are tender.

5 Return the turkey to the pot; add the wine or broth, increase the heat to high and bring to a boil. Stir in the tomatoes and their juices, and the tomato paste, and bring to a boil. Reduce the heat to low, cover the pot and simmer the sauce, stirring occasionally, for 30 minutes.

6 Uncover the pot and simmer for 15 minutes longer, or until the sauce has thickened and the flavors are blended.

Per serving 87 calories, 2.6 g. fat, 0.4 g. saturated fat, 18 mg. cholesterol, 246 mg. sodium **Serves 32 (makes 16 cups)**

PASTA CHOICES
rigatoni, ziti or penne rigate (ridged penne), radiatore, spaghetti or perciatelli

VARIATIONS
Substitute chicken breast or lean beef or pork for all or some of the turkey.

Newfangled Chili Sauce: Add rinsed and drained canned kidney beans, along with chili powder and hot sauce to taste, to Neo-Classic Bolognese Sauce. Serve over pasta or rice.

OTHER USES
Use Neo-Classic Bolognese Sauce to make lasagna or other baked pasta dishes.

For a quick soup, thin 2 cups of the sauce with 2 to 3 cups of broth; add some pastina (tiny pasta shapes), diced carrots and diced celery, and simmer until the pasta and vegetables are tender.

TIPS
Spoon the sauce into heavy zip-closure bags and press out excess air; seal the bags and lay them flat in the freezer. Once frozen, they can be stacked. For individual servings, freeze the sauce in small yogurt containers.

BASIC WHITE SAUCE

❧ ❧ ❧

3 cups 1% low-fat milk

2 cups defatted reduced-sodium chicken broth

2 whole garlic cloves, peeled

1 bay leaf, preferably imported

½ teaspoon dried thyme

6 whole black peppercorns

2 tablespoons unsalted butter or margarine

⅓ cup all-purpose flour

¼ teaspoon salt

¼ teaspoon freshly ground pepper

1 Combine the milk, broth, garlic cloves, bay leaf, thyme and peppercorns in a heavy medium saucepan, and bring to a boil over high heat, watching carefully so it doesn't boil over. Remove from the heat, cover and let stand for 15 minutes to infuse the liquid with the seasonings. Strain into a large measuring cup.

2 Melt the butter or margarine in a large heavy saucepan over medium heat. Sprinkle in the flour and cook, stirring constantly, for 1 minute, or until the flour is completely incorporated and the mixture is bubbly. Pour in the milk mixture, whisking constantly. (The sauce will be very thick.) Remove the pan from the heat, cover and let stand for 2 minutes (this will help to make a smoother sauce).

3 Return the pan to medium-high heat and bring to a boil, stirring constantly. Use a whisk at first, then switch to a wooden spoon. Reduce the heat to medium-low and simmer, stirring frequently, for 8 to 10 minutes, or until the sauce is thickened and smooth. Stir in the salt and pepper.

Per serving 90 calories, 4 g. fat, 2.4 g. saturated fat, 11 mg. cholesterol, 274 mg. sodium **Serves 8 (makes 4 cups)**

PASTA CHOICES

For Pasta Alfredo: fettuccine, linguine, tagliatelle or spinach noodles. For Spinach and Clam Sauce: spaghetti or spaghettini. For Creamy Pasta Primavera: shells or ziti. For Pasta with Prosciutto and Peas: regular or spinach linguine. For Oregano-Tomato Sauce: fusilli or cavatappi.

VARIATIONS

Basic White Sauce is intended as a base for the following sauces, each made with 2 cups of hot Basic White Sauce:

Pasta Alfredo: Add 1 ounce grated Parmesan, ⅛ to ¼ teaspoon freshly ground black pepper and a large pinch of nutmeg (preferably freshly grated).

Spinach and Clam Sauce: Thaw and squeeze dry half a 10-ounce package of frozen chopped spinach. Sauté 2 crushed garlic cloves in 1½ teaspoons oil. Stir in the spinach, 1 small can drained minced clams and ⅛ teaspoon pepper, and cook until heated through. Add the Basic White Sauce and bring to a boil.

Creamy Pasta Primavera: Add 4 cups steamed fresh vegetables to Basic White Sauce and simmer together until the sauce and vegetables are heated through. Stir in ½ ounce grated Parmesan and ¼ cup coarsely chopped fresh basil.

Pasta with Prosciutto and Peas: Add 2 ounces diced prosciutto (or smoked turkey), 1 cup frozen peas and a large pinch of ground red pepper to the Basic White Sauce. Simmer until heated through.

Oregano-Tomato Sauce: Warm 1 teaspoon olive oil in a medium skillet. Add 1 cup diced fresh tomatoes and 2 minced garlic cloves, and sauté for 2 to 3 minutes, or just until hot. Stir in the Basic White Sauce and bring to a boil. Season with 2 tablespoons coarsely chopped fresh oregano, ¼ teaspoon freshly ground pepper and 2 tablespoons grated Parmesan.

ITALIAN HERB SEASONING MIX

❧ ❧ ❧

5 medium bay leaves, preferably imported

2 teaspoons dried rosemary

2 teaspoons fennel seeds

¼ cup dried basil

2 tablespoons dried oregano

3 tablespoons dried thyme

½ teaspoon freshly ground black pepper

1 Put the bay leaves, rosemary and fennel seeds in a small food processor or a clean coffee grinder and process until the herbs are finely ground. Pour into a small bowl.

2 Add the basil, oregano, thyme and pepper, and stir to mix. Transfer the mixture to a jar with a tight-fitting lid and store in a cool, dry place.

Makes ½ cup

USES
Add 1½ teaspoons of Italian Herb Seasoning Mix to two 8-ounce cans of no-salt-added tomato sauce for a flavorful pasta sauce.

Use the herb mix to spice up canned tomato or tomato-rice soup.

Add ½ teaspoon of Italian Herb Seasoning Mix to ½ cup of your favorite vinaigrette; use it on salads or chilled cooked vegetables.

Add ½ teaspoon of Italian Herb Seasoning Mix to ⅓ cup of a lemon- or lime-juice-based marinade for poultry or fish.

While you cook 8 ounces of pasta, heat 1 tablespoon oil, add 1 or 2 cloves crushed garlic and ½ teaspoon Italian Herb Seasoning Mix; toss the pasta with the flavored oil.

Before baking or broiling, rub 2 pounds of skinless bone-in chicken pieces with 1 tablespoon lemon juice, ¼ teaspoon salt, 1 teaspoon grated lemon zest and 1½ teaspoons Italian Herb Seasoning Mix.

TIPS
Be sure the herbs and spices you use are strongly fragrant: The seasoning mix will be no better than the ingredients you start out with. Crumble each herb between your fingers and sniff it: If the aroma is weak, it's time to buy a new jar. Dried herbs should be stored in a cool, dark place in tightly closed containers—a spot over the stove, though convenient, is not the best place for the spice rack.

After making the mixture, transfer it from the bowl to a jar by making a funnel out of a small sheet of paper.

PASTA STRANDS

These pastas are made by forcing dough through metal plates perforated with holes of various shapes, or by cutting flat sheets of dough. Rather than breaking long pasta to fit the pot, place one end of the pasta in the boiling water and push the rest into the pot as soon as the bottom part softens a bit.

Capelli d'angelo (angel hair), at left, are the thinnest pasta strands. Traditionally served in broth, angel hair also works well with light-textured sauces.

These broad, medium and fine egg noodles are popular in Eastern European, German and Pennsylvania-German cooking. Serve them in soups, with mild-flavored, creamy sauces, or bake them into sweet noodle puddings for dessert.

Vermicelli (the name means "little worms") also comes in coiled nests. Use it like angel hair, or break the pasta up and add it to soup.

At left is spaghettini, and below, whole-wheat spaghetti. Both can be used with a wide variety of sauces, or in casseroles.

Perciatelli (below), also called bucatini, is a thick, hollow spaghetti. Serve these sturdy strands with robust, chunky sauces.

Fusilli means "springs." This is dried and fresh long fusilli, in plain, spinach and tomato varieties. Pair it with a sauce that has a bit of body—both fusilli and linguine can be slippery and hard to eat when served with sauces that are thin or oily.

The narrow flat strands above are linguine, which means "little tongues." Spinach linguine (on the left) retains a slight flavor of that vegetable; whole-wheat linguine (on the right) has, like all whole-wheat pastas, a chewier, more substantial texture and a more assertive flavor than regular pasta.

Dried fettuccine (the name means "little ribbons") is a versatile and popular egg pasta. Use it with creamy-textured sauces or flavorful pesto; toss the pasta with julienne-cut or shredded vegetables that echo its shape.

Fresh fettuccine is widely available; tomato and plain are shown here. Plain and spinach fettuccine are sometimes cooked together to make a dish called "hay and straw." You can apply this idea to any combination of pasta colors.

These are coils of fresh plain, tomato and spinach capellini, a slightly thicker version of angel hair. Be sure to check for doneness early on when cooking fresh pasta: Fresh capellini cooks in just two to three minutes.

PASTA SHAPES

Pasta comes in hundreds of different shapes, giving you countless mealtime options. Suit the pasta to the sauce: Hollow or convoluted shapes such as ziti catch morsels of vegetables or meat in a chunky sauce; fusilli and similar twists and coils add interest to smooth sauces. Stuffed pastas are usually served simply, with herbed olive oil or grated cheese; a light tomato sauce, vegetable sauce or pesto is tasty with these pastas, too.

Each piece of rigatoni, above, is a satisfying mouthful. This sturdy pasta can stand up to an assertive sauce with big chunks of meat or poultry.

Most children love pasta, and a variety of amusing shapes helps pique their appetites. This "sunshine" macaroni is great to use for pasta salads or to serve with a simple sauce.

Macaroni rigati are medium-sized ridged tubes. They're perfect for baking in a casserole or tossing with a spicy tomato sauce.

Tiny pastas, such as this orzo ("barley"), are traditionally used in soup. Orzo can also be served as you would rice, as a base for a richly flavored, stewlike sauce.

Use ziti (the name means "bridegrooms") with thick or chunky sauces.

Short fusilli bucati, right, are hollow "springs" that are good with vegetable sauces and in salads.

This pasta shape may be called rotelle, rotini, fusilli, eliche—or simply twists. These tricolor twists are attractive in a pasta-and-vegetable salad.

Combine penne— "quills"—with other ingredients that echo its shape: cut-up asparagus or green beans, julienned carrots, or strips of chicken, for example. Spinach penne is shown here.

Cavatelli—the name means "little hollows"— catch and hold bits of meat and vegetables as well as sauce, so you enjoy the full flavor of the dish with every forkful.

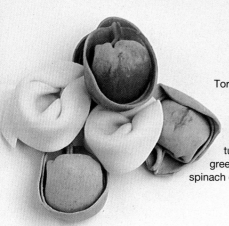

Tortelloni are larger versions of cappelletti (below); they are often filled with a mixture of ricotta and greens, such as spinach or Swiss chard.

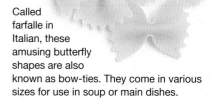

Ravioli, the most familiar stuffed pasta, is most frequently found in meat or ricotta cheese versions. But gourmet shops also offer ravioli filled with mushrooms (or truffles), broccoli rabe, lobster or a savory pumpkin mixture. The ravioli shown here are made with spinach and tomato dough.

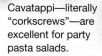

Cavatappi—literally "corkscrews"—are excellent for party pasta salads.

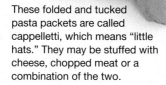

These folded and tucked pasta packets are called cappelletti, which means "little hats." They may be stuffed with cheese, chopped meat or a combination of the two.

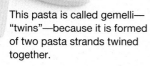

This pasta is called gemelli—"twins"—because it is formed of two pasta strands twined together.

Called farfalle in Italian, these amusing butterfly shapes are also known as bow-ties. They come in various sizes for use in soup or main dishes.

Supposedly modeled after a European heating device, tightly furled radiatore ("radiators") are among the best pastas for salads.

The popular shells, or conchiglie, come in many sizes and colors. These are tinted with beet and spinach.

American children grow up with "wagon wheels," but this pasta shape originated in Sicily, where it is called ruote.

Pasta with Poultry

❧ ❧ ❧

QUICK-COOKING CHICKEN

AND TURKEY TURN PASTA

INTO HEARTY DINNERS, SATISFYING

SALADS AND MORE

PEPPER-SAUCED PENNE WITH SAUSAGE

3 medium red bell peppers, halved and cored

1 green bell pepper, halved and cored

1 yellow bell pepper, halved and cored

1 medium onion, sliced

6 ounces hot or sweet turkey sausage, cut into ½-inch slices

3 garlic cloves, sliced

1 teaspoon olive oil

⅓ cup defatted reduced-sodium chicken broth

8 ounces penne pasta

¼ teaspoon freshly ground black pepper

Readily available turkey sausage comes in both hot and sweet varieties, just as pork sausage does. For this recipe, use either one alone or a combination of the two. For step-by-step photographs showing how to roast peppers, see page 49.

1 Bring a large covered pot of water to a boil over high heat. Preheat the broiler. Spray the broiler-pan rack with no-stick spray.

2 While the water comes to a boil, arrange the bell peppers and onions on the prepared broiler rack and broil 4 to 5 inches from the heat, turning once, for 10 minutes, or until the peppers and onions are tender and lightly charred. Transfer the broiled vegetables to a plate.

3 Arrange the sausage in a single layer on the broiler-pan rack and broil, turning once, for 10 minutes, or until the sausage is lightly browned and cooked through. Remove from the heat.

4 While the sausage is cooking, in a small skillet combine the sliced garlic and the oil, and sauté, stirring constantly, for 1 to 2 minutes, or just until the garlic is lightly browned. Transfer the garlic to a plate.

5 Peel or scrape the charred skin from the peppers. Place the 3 red peppers, the onion, browned garlic and the broth in a food processor and process until puréed. Cut the green and yellow peppers into thin strips; set aside.

6 Add the pasta to the boiling water, return to a boil and cook for 10 to 12 minutes or according to package directions until al dente. Reserving ½ cup of the cooking liquid, drain the pasta in a colander.

7 Combine the red pepper purée, reserved cooking liquid, sausage and black pepper in the pasta cooking pot and bring to a boil over high heat; cook for 1 to 2 minutes to heat the sausage through. Add the pasta and roasted pepper strips, and toss until coated with sauce.

Preparation time 11 minutes • **Total time** 40 minutes • **Per serving** 337 calories, 6.9 g. fat (18% of calories), 2 g. saturated fat, 26 mg. cholesterol, 322 mg. sodium, 3.5 g. dietary fiber, 38 mg. calcium, 3 mg. iron, 142 mg. vitamin C, 2 mg. beta-carotene
Serves 4

❧ ❧ ❧

Preceding pages: Rigatoni with Herbed Chicken (recipe on page 41).

SESAME NOODLES WITH LEMON CHICKEN

8 **ounces thin-sliced chicken cutlets**

1 **tablespoon plus 1 teaspoon reduced-sodium soy sauce**

1 **tablespoon plus 1 teaspoon fresh lemon juice**

1½ **teaspoons grated fresh ginger**

¼ **teaspoon freshly ground black pepper**

8 **ounces spaghetti**

2 **tablespoons reduced-fat peanut butter**

2 **tablespoons defatted chicken broth**

1 **teaspoon dark sesame oil**

¼ **teaspoon crushed red pepper flakes**

1 **cup julienne-cut unpeeled kirby cucumbers**

½ **cup shredded carrots**

¼ **cup diagonally sliced scallions**

To julienne the cucumbers, cut off the ends and then halve the cucumbers crosswise. Quarter each half lengthwise, then cut it into thin sticks.

Szechuan restaurants continue to flourish in the United States, with sesame noodles one of their most popular dishes. Chinese cooks use a rich golden sesame paste, but here, a mixture of peanut butter and fragrant dark sesame oil produces a remarkably similar flavor. The noodles can be served either warm or chilled.

1 Bring a large covered pot of water to a boil over high heat. Meanwhile, preheat the broiler and spray a jelly-roll pan with no-stick spray.

2 Arrange the chicken in a single layer in the prepared pan and drizzle with 2 teaspoons of the soy sauce, 1 teaspoon of the lemon juice, 1 teaspoon of the ginger and the black pepper. Rub the seasonings into the surface; cover and let stand while you cook the pasta.

3 Add the pasta to the boiling water, return to a boil and cook for 8 to 10 minutes or according to package directions until al dente. Reserving ¼ cup of the cooking liquid, drain the pasta in a colander.

4 Broil the chicken 4 to 5 inches from the heat for 6 to 7 minutes, or until the chicken is lightly browned and cooked through. Remove from the broiler.

5 In a small bowl, whisk together 3 tablespoons of the reserved pasta cooking liquid, the peanut butter, broth, sesame oil, red pepper flakes, the remaining 2 teaspoons soy sauce, remaining 1 tablespoon lemon juice and remaining ½ teaspoon ginger.

6 Place the pasta in a serving bowl. Cut the chicken into strips and add the chicken and any juices from the pan to the pasta. Pour the peanut sauce over the chicken, add the cucumber, carrots and scallions, and toss to mix. If the pasta seems a bit dry, add the remaining tablespoon of pasta cooking liquid or a little boiling water.

Preparation time 20 minutes • **Total time** 40 minutes • **Per serving** 350 calories, 6.1 g. fat (16% of calories), 1 g. saturated fat, 33 mg. cholesterol, 313 mg. sodium, 2.5 g. dietary fiber, 31 mg. calcium, 3 mg. iron, 7 mg. vitamin C, 2.4 mg. beta-carotene **Serves 4**

CHICKEN CACCIATORE PASTA

1 tablespoon extra-virgin olive oil

1 large onion, sliced

3 garlic cloves, minced

½ teaspoon dried thyme, crumbled

½ teaspoon freshly ground black pepper

1 bay leaf, preferably imported

¼ teaspoon dried rosemary, crumbled

⅛ teaspoon salt

10 ounces small fresh mushrooms, quartered

2 tablespoons defatted chicken broth

1 can (16 ounces) crushed tomatoes in purée

2 tablespoons dry white wine (optional)

8 ounces cavatelli or other macaroni

8 ounces boneless, skinless chicken breast halves, cut into ½-inch chunks

The word *cacciatore* (hunter) suggests the sort of hearty dish that a hunter might put together after a day in the forests and fields. The main ingredient would be game (here updated with chicken), and the robust accompaniments traditionally include onions, tomatoes, mushrooms, garlic and wine.

1 Bring a large covered pot of water to a boil over high heat.

2 Meanwhile, heat the oil in a large, heavy skillet over high heat. Add the onions and garlic, and sauté for 3 to 4 minutes, or until the onions are tender and very lightly browned. Stir in the thyme, pepper, bay leaf, rosemary and salt, and cook, stirring constantly, for 30 seconds.

3 Stir in the mushrooms and broth and bring to a boil. Reduce the heat to medium-high and cook, stirring frequently, for 4 to 5 minutes, or until the mushrooms are tender. Stir in the tomatoes and the wine (if using), and return to a boil. Reduce the heat to low, cover and simmer for 10 minutes to blend the flavors.

4 Add the pasta to the boiling water, return to a boil and cook for 10 to 12 minutes or according to package directions until al dente. Drain in a colander.

5 Add the chicken to the sauce; increase the heat to medium, cover and simmer, stirring frequently, for 5 to 8 minutes longer, or until the chicken is cooked through. Remove and discard the bay leaf.

6 Transfer the pasta to a warmed serving bowl, spoon the sauce over the pasta and toss to mix.

Preparation time 15 minutes • **Total time** 45 minutes • **Per serving** 378 calories, 5.6 g. fat (13% of calories), 0.9 g. saturated fat, 33 mg. cholesterol, 326 mg. sodium, 3.2 g. dietary fiber, 84 mg. calcium, 4 mg. iron, 26 mg. vitamin C, 0.5 mg. beta-carotene • **Serves 4**

SMOKED TURKEY CARBONARA

8 ounces linguine

8 ounces asparagus, sliced diagonally into 1-inch pieces

2 large eggs

3 large egg whites

¼ cup skim milk

2 tablespoons grated Parmesan cheese

2 tablespoons chopped fresh Italian parsley

½ teaspoon freshly ground black pepper

⅛ teaspoon salt

Large pinch of ground nutmeg, preferably freshly grated

Large pinch of ground red pepper

3 ounces smoked turkey, cut into julienne

1 tablespoon olive oil

The term *carbonara* describes dishes cooked with bacon or ham; the best-known of these dishes is *pasta alla carbonara*, a luxuriously rich creation that calls for pancetta (an Italian cured bacon), Parmesan or Romano cheese, heavy cream—and one whole egg per serving. For this version, smoked turkey stands in for pancetta and skim milk substitutes for cream; two eggs (combined with two egg whites, which are virtually fat-free) serve four.

1 Bring a large covered pot of water to a boil over high heat. Add the pasta to the boiling water, return to a boil and cook, stirring frequently, for 9 to 11 minutes or according to package directions. Two minutes before the pasta is done, add the asparagus and cook until the asparagus is crisp-tender and the pasta is al dente. Drain the pasta and asparagus in a colander and rinse briefly under cold running water; drain again.

2 In a large bowl, whisk together the eggs, egg whites, milk, Parmesan, parsley, black pepper, salt, nutmeg and red pepper until well blended. Stir in the turkey. Add the pasta and asparagus, and toss, using 2 spoons, until the spaghetti is coated with the egg mixture.

3 In a large no-stick skillet, warm the oil over high heat. Add the pasta mixture and cook, tossing constantly with 2 wooden spoons, for 2 to 3 minutes, or until the eggs have set into small clumps and the pasta is hot.

Preparation time 10 minutes • **Total time** 20 minutes • **Per serving** 347 calories, 8.5 g. fat (22% of calories), 2.2 g. saturated fat, 120 mg. cholesterol, 428 mg. sodium, 2.1 g. dietary fiber, 103 mg. calcium, 3 mg. iron, 21 mg. vitamin C, 0.5 mg. beta-carotene • **Serves 4**

Intensely fragrant freshly grated nutmeg makes a tremendous difference in both savory and sweet dishes. This miniature grater is specially made for nutmeg.

KITCHEN TIPS

Cooking the asparagus in the same pot with the pasta is a time-saver, but be sure to add the asparagus gradually so the water does not stop boiling.

MARKET AND PANTRY

Smoked turkey, cured over flavorful woods such as mesquite or apple, is widely available. Keep it well wrapped so its assertive aroma does not permeate other foods.

TURKEY TETRAZZINI

8 ounces wide egg noodles

1½ cups defatted reduced-sodium chicken broth

1 cup 1% low-fat milk

3 tablespoons cornstarch

½ teaspoon freshly ground black pepper

½ teaspoon dried thyme, crumbled

⅛ teaspoon salt

4 tablespoons grated Parmesan cheese

1½ teaspoons dry sherry (optional)

1 tablespoon unsalted butter or margarine

8 ounces fresh mushrooms, sliced

¾ cup thinly sliced scallions

4 ounces skinless roast turkey breast, cut into matchstick strips about the same length as the noodles

The name of Italian opera diva Luisa Tetrazzini lives on in the baked pasta dish created in her honor. An admiring chef devised a dinner of spaghetti, chicken and mushrooms in a sherried cream sauce, topped with Parmesan and baked until golden. Turkey is often substituted for chicken in the dish; to lighten this particular rendition, a mixture of low-fat milk and cornstarch takes the place of the cream sauce.

1 Preheat the oven to 450°. Spray a 9 x 9-inch or 11 x 7-inch baking dish with no-stick spray.

2 Bring a large covered pot of water to a boil over high heat. Add the noodles to the boiling water, return to a boil and cook for 5 to 6 minutes (the noodles should be slightly underdone). Drain in a colander and rinse briefly under gently running cold water to keep the noodles from sticking; drain again.

3 Meanwhile, in a medium saucepan, whisk together the broth, milk, cornstarch, pepper, thyme and salt. Bring to a boil over high heat, whisking constantly. Cook, stirring, until the sauce is thickened and smooth. Remove from the heat and stir in 3 tablespoons of the Parmesan and the sherry (if using).

4 In the pasta cooking pot, melt the butter or margarine over medium-high heat. Add the mushrooms and scallions, and sauté for 2 to 4 minutes, or until the mushrooms are tender (the pan will be dry at first; keep stirring and the mushrooms will release their liquid). Remove the pot from the heat and stir in the noodles, sauce and turkey. Toss until mixed, then transfer to the prepared pan.

5 Sprinkle the surface with the remaining 1 tablespoon Parmesan. Bake for 15 minutes, or until the sauce is bubbly and the top of the casserole is lightly browned.

Preparation time 10 minutes • **Total time** 45 minutes • **Per serving** 397 calories, 10 g. fat (23% of calories), 4.3 g. saturated fat, 91 mg. cholesterol, 493 mg. sodium, 2.8 g. dietary fiber, 206 mg. calcium, 4 mg. iron, 6 mg. vitamin C, 0.2 mg. beta-carotene • **Serves 4**

TURKISH-STYLE PASTA WITH CHICKEN

1 cup plain nonfat yogurt

¾ cup defatted reduced-sodium chicken broth

8 ounces boneless, skinless chicken breast halves, cut crosswise into ½-inch strips

6 ounces wide egg noodles

8 ounces green beans, trimmed and cut into 1-inch lengths

2 medium kirby cucumbers, scrubbed, trimmed and thinly sliced

⅓ cup finely chopped red onions

1½ teaspoons ground cumin

¼ teaspoon ground coriander

¼ teaspoon turmeric

¼ teaspoon freshly ground black pepper

¼ teaspoon salt

⅛ teaspoon ground red pepper

The refreshing combination of cucumbers and yogurt appears on tables all over the Near East and Asia Minor, often as chilled soups or creamy sauces. Here, yogurt (briefly drained to thicken it) is mixed with thinly sliced cucumbers, chopped onions, cumin, coriander and turmeric to serve as a sauce for egg noodles, poached chicken strips and green beans.

1 Bring a large covered pot of water to a boil over high heat.

2 Meanwhile, spoon the yogurt into a cheesecloth-lined strainer suspended over a bowl and let drain for 15 minutes.

3 While the yogurt drains, bring the broth to a boil in a covered, deep, medium skillet over high heat. Add the chicken breasts, reduce the heat to medium-low, cover and simmer, turning often, for 3 to 4 minutes, or until the chicken is cooked through. Using a slotted spoon, transfer the chicken to a plate; cover loosely to keep it moist. Boil the broth over high heat for 7 to 8 minutes, or until it is reduced to about 1 tablespoon of caramel-colored syrup.

4 Add the noodles and green beans to the boiling water; return to a boil and cook for 5 to 6 minutes or according to package directions until the noodles are al dente and the beans are tender. Drain the noodles and beans in a colander; transfer to a warmed serving bowl.

5 In a small bowl, mix the yogurt, cucumbers, onions, cumin, coriander, turmeric, black pepper, salt and red pepper. Pour the sauce over the noodles, add the chicken and reduced broth, and toss well.

Preparation time 15 minutes • **Total time** 35 minutes • **Per serving** 290 calories, 3 g. fat (10% of calories), 0.7 g. saturated fat, 74 mg. cholesterol, 351 mg. sodium, 2.7 g. dietary fiber, 169 mg. calcium, 4 mg. iron, 13 mg. vitamin C, 0.3 mg. beta-carotene • **Serves 4**

ON THE MENU
Precede this meal with a Near-Eastern appetizer, such as a dip made of roasted eggplant and garlic served with crisp baked pita triangles.

KITCHEN TIPS
The slicing slot on a metal grater—if it is sufficiently sharp—can be used to slice the cucumbers. Otherwise, cut them by hand or with a mechanical slicer.

FETTUCCINE WITH TURKEY "SAUSAGE"

8 ounces boneless, skinless turkey breast, cut into chunks

½ teaspoon freshly ground black pepper

½ teaspoon dried thyme

¼ teaspoon dried sage or ¾ teaspoon minced fresh sage

¼ teaspoon fennel seed

¼ teaspoon crushed red pepper flakes

2 teaspoons olive oil

1 large onion, chopped

2 garlic cloves, minced

¾ cup defatted reduced-sodium chicken broth

1 can (16 ounces) whole tomatoes in purée, finely chopped in a food processor or blender

6 ounces fettuccine

As the turkey cooks, its color will change from translucent pink to opaque white.

resh Italian sausage, an earthy blend of chopped pork, pepper, garlic, sage and fennel, comes in sweet and hot varieties, the latter spiked with red pepper. For a low-fat meal with all the flavor of Italian sausage, ground turkey is combined with the traditional seasonings, cooked with tomatoes and served over fettuccine.

1 Bring a large covered pot of water to a boil over high heat.

2 Meanwhile, process the turkey in a food processor until finely ground. Add the black pepper, thyme, sage, fennel seeds and red pepper flakes, and pulse until blended.

3 Heat the oil in a large, heavy skillet over medium-high heat. Add the onions and garlic, and stir to blend with the oil. Add 2 tablespoons of the broth and sauté for 4 to 5 minutes, or until the onions are tender. Stir in the turkey mixture and 2 tablespoons more broth, and cook, stirring to break up the clumps of turkey, for 2 to 3 minutes, or until the turkey turns white.

4 Stir in the tomatoes and the remaining ½ cup broth and bring to a boil. Reduce the heat to medium-low, cover and simmer, stirring occasionally, for 15 minutes, or until the flavors are blended.

5 Meanwhile, add the pasta to the boiling water, return to a boil and cook for 9 to 11 minutes or according to package directions until al dente. Drain in a colander and transfer to a warmed serving bowl. Pour the sauce over the pasta and toss to mix.

Preparation time 15 minutes • **Total time** 45 minutes • **Per serving** 305 calories, 4.7 g. fat (14% of calories), 0.8 g. saturated fat, 76 mg. cholesterol, 339 mg. sodium, 2.1 g. dietary fiber, 80 mg. calcium, 3 mg. iron, 22 mg. vitamin C, 0.5 mg. beta-carotene • **Serves 4**

MARKET AND PANTRY
It's best to grind turkey breast yourself rather than buying ground turkey, which may contain dark meat and skin. You can also have the butcher grind a piece of skinless turkey breast for you. Use ground turkey within a day of purchase, as it is more perishable than uncut poultry.

ON THE MENU
For dessert, offer sliced cantaloupe or honeydew with fresh figs.

Fusilli, Turkey and Orange Salad

8 ounces spinach fusilli

2 navel oranges

2 tablespoons frozen orange juice concentrate

2 tablespoons defatted chicken broth

1 tablespoon extra-virgin olive oil

2 teaspoons balsamic vinegar

¼ teaspoon salt

¼ teaspoon freshly ground black pepper

⅛ teaspoon crushed red pepper flakes

8 ounces thin turkey-breast slices, cut into ½-inch-wide strips

½ cup thinly shredded basil leaves

1½ cups thinly sliced celery or fennel

6 kalamata or ripe olives, sliced off pits

The combination of oranges and olives is distinctly Mediterranean, and orange-and-olive salads are popular in Italy, especially around Rome. Kalamata olives, used here, are available in many supermarkets. Rather than trying to halve and pit the olives, use a sharp paring knife to shave the flesh from the pits.

1 Bring a large covered pot of water to a boil over high heat. Preheat the broiler and spray a jelly-roll pan with no-stick spray.

2 Add the pasta to the boiling water, return to a boil and cook for 10 to 12 minutes or according to package directions until al dente. Drain in a colander and rinse briefly under cold running water; drain again.

3 Meanwhile, with a serrated knife, pare the peel and white pith from the oranges. Working over a medium bowl, cut out the orange sections between the membranes, letting the sections fall into the bowl. Squeeze the juice from the membranes over the oranges. Pour the juice into a salad bowl.

4 To the juice, add the orange juice concentrate, broth, oil, vinegar, ⅛ teaspoon salt, ⅛ teaspoon of the black pepper and the red pepper flakes, and whisk with a fork until blended; set aside.

5 Place the turkey strips in the prepared pan and toss with 2 tablespoons of the basil and the remaining ⅛ teaspoon salt and remaining ⅛ teaspoon black pepper. Arrange the turkey strips in a single layer and broil 3 to 4 inches from the heat for 4 to 5 minutes, turning the pieces once, until cooked through.

6 Add the pasta to the bowl of dressing and toss gently. Add the turkey (and any juices that have collected in the pan), the oranges, celery or fennel, olives and the remaining 6 tablespoons basil, and toss gently to coat.

Preparation time 25 minutes • **Total time** 40 minutes • **Per serving** 385 calories, 5.7 g. fat (13% of calories), 0.9 g. saturated fat, 47 mg. cholesterol, 307 mg. sodium, 8.7 g. dietary fiber, 143 mg. calcium, 4 mg. iron, 57 mg. vitamin C, 0.3 mg. beta-carotene • **Serves 4**

TEX-MEX PASTA BAKE

1 can (14½ ounces) no-salt-added stewed tomatoes

1 can (8 ounces) no-salt-added tomato sauce

½ cup hot or medium salsa

1 can (4 ounces) chopped green chilies, rinsed and drained

1 tablespoon fresh lime juice

1¼ teaspoons ground cumin

¼ teaspoon dried oregano, crumbled

8 ounces rigatoni pasta

1 can (10½ ounces) pinto or red kidney beans, rinsed and drained

½ cup frozen corn kernels

3 ounces skinless roast turkey, diced

2 ounces Monterey Jack cheese, shredded

Here's a dish for hearty appetites. It's a casserole of rigatoni with chunks of turkey, beans and corn kernels in a spicy tomato sauce, topped with velvety Monterey Jack cheese. For even more Tex-Mex flavor, make this pasta dish with pepper-jack cheese, which is Monterey Jack flecked with bits of jalapeño.

1 Preheat the oven to 450°. Spray a 9 x 13-inch baking dish with no-stick spray. Bring a large covered pot of water to a boil over high heat.

2 Meanwhile, in a medium saucepan combine the stewed tomatoes, tomato sauce, salsa, chilies, lime juice, cumin and oregano, and bring to a boil over high heat. Reduce the heat to medium, cover and simmer, stirring occasionally, for 5 minutes.

3 While the sauce simmers, add the pasta to the boiling water, return to a boil and cook for 11 to 13 minutes or according to package directions until al dente. Drain in a colander.

4 While the pasta cooks, add the beans, corn and turkey to the sauce, and bring to a boil; remove the pan from the heat.

5 Return the drained rigatoni to the pasta cooking pot; add the sauce and toss to mix. Transfer to the prepared baking dish and sprinkle with the cheese. Bake for 10 minutes, or until the cheese is melted and the sauce is bubbly.

Preparation time 12 minutes • **Total time** 45 minutes • **Per serving** 415 calories, 6.7 g. fat (14% of calories), 2.8 g. saturated fat, 33 mg. cholesterol, 474 mg. sodium, 7.4 g. dietary fiber, 176 mg. calcium, 5 mg. iron, 47 mg. vitamin C, 1 mg. beta-carotene • **Serves 4**

ON THE MENU
Serve a salad of grated carrots and jícama, a Mexican tuber that looks something like a turnip and tastes like a cross between water chestnuts and apples. Pare jícama with a swivel-bladed vegetable peeler before grating it; dress the salad with lime juice and sprinkle it with chopped cilantro.

HEADSTART
Make the tomato sauce through step 2 in advance. Bring it to a simmer before adding the beans, corn kernels and turkey.

NUTRITION NOTE
Beans and other legumes are excellent sources of both soluble and insoluble fiber.

THAI CHICKEN AND NOODLES

1¼ cups loosely packed cilantro sprigs

¼ cup defatted chicken broth

2 tablespoons fresh lime juice

1 tablespoon plus 1 teaspoon reduced-sodium soy sauce

1 tablespoon grated fresh ginger

2 teaspoons granulated sugar

1 teaspoon dark sesame oil

½ teaspoon crushed red pepper flakes

1 garlic clove, peeled

8 ounces thin-sliced chicken cutlets, cut into strips

8 ounces thin egg noodles or vermicelli

1 large red bell pepper, cut into thin strips

½ cup grated radishes

Use the fine side of a grater for shredding pungent fresh ginger. You need not peel the ginger before grating it.

T hai restaurants are still a relative novelty in the United States, and some Thai ingredients, such as spicy galanga root and citrus-scented lemongrass, are available only in specialty stores. However, these exotic flavors can be approximated, as they are here, with ginger and lime juice.

1 Bring a large covered pot of water to a boil over high heat.

2 Meanwhile, combine the cilantro, broth, lime juice, soy sauce, ginger, sugar, oil and red pepper flakes in a food processor. With the machine running, drop the garlic clove through the feed tube and process until puréed. Put the chicken in a medium bowl, add ¼ cup of the cilantro sauce and toss to mix well. Cover and let stand at room temperature for 10 minutes.

3 Transfer the chicken mixture to a medium no-stick skillet. Cook over medium-high heat, tossing frequently, for 3 to 4 minutes, or until the chicken is cooked through. Remove the pan from the heat.

4 Add the pasta to the boiling water, return to a boil and cook for 2 to 4 minutes or according to package directions until al dente. One minute before the pasta is done, stir in the bell pepper strips. Drain the pasta and peppers in a colander; transfer to a serving bowl.

5 Add the remaining cilantro sauce and the chicken mixture to the noodles, and toss to coat. Scatter the radishes on top.

Preparation time 20 minutes • **Total time** 40 minutes • **Per serving** 317 calories, 4.5 g. fat (13% of calories), 0.8 g. saturated fat, 87 mg. cholesterol, 316 mg. sodium, 2.2 g. dietary fiber, 39 mg. calcium, 3 mg. iron, 55 mg. vitamin C, 1 mg. beta-carotene
Serves 4

MARKET AND PANTRY
Fragrant dark sesame oil, made from toasted sesame seeds, is essential in many Asian cuisines; it is most often used as a seasoning rather than as a cooking oil. it can be found in Asian food stores,

gourmet shops and some supermarkets. Do not substitute light sesame oil.

ON THE MENU
For a light first course, serve bowls of broth flavored with ginger and scallions.

RIGATONI WITH HERBED CHICKEN

8 ounces boneless, skinless chicken breast halves, cut into ½-inch chunks

3 garlic cloves, crushed

½ teaspoon dried basil, crumbled

¼ teaspoon dried thyme, crumbled

¼ teaspoon fennel seeds

⅛ teaspoon freshly ground black pepper

⅛ teaspoon crushed red pepper flakes

2 teaspoons extra-virgin olive oil

2 cans (14½ ounces each) no-salt-added tomatoes in juice, coarsely chopped, 1 cup of juice reserved

1 tablespoon no-salt-added tomato paste

8 ounces rigatoni pasta

3 tablespoons chopped fresh basil or 2 tablespoons chopped fresh Italian parsley

½ cup part-skim ricotta cheese

Ricotta cheese often goes into the filling for stuffed pastas such as manicotti and ravioli, but it can also be used with quick sauce-topped pastas. Here, part-skim ricotta—which is lower in fat but richer in calcium than whole-milk ricotta—tops a plate of sturdy rigatoni with a chunky chicken and tomato sauce.

1 Bring a large covered pot of water to a boil over high heat.

2 Put the chicken in a medium bowl; add the garlic, basil, thyme, fennel seeds, black pepper and red pepper flakes, and mix well.

3 In a large no-stick skillet, warm the oil over high heat until very hot. Add the chicken chunks, and sauté for 2 to 3 minutes, or until the chicken turns light golden. Stir in the tomatoes and the reserved juice, and the tomato paste, and bring to a boil, stirring to get up any browned bits that have adhered to the bottom of the skillet. Reduce the heat to medium-low and simmer, stirring frequently, for 10 minutes, or until the sauce has thickened slightly.

4 Meanwhile, add the pasta to the boiling water, return to a boil and cook for 12 to 14 minutes or according to package directions until al dente. Reserving ¼ cup of the pasta cooking liquid, drain the rigatoni in a colander.

5 Stir the basil or parsley into the tomato and chicken mixture. Combine the rigatoni and the reserved cooking liquid in a warmed serving bowl. Pour the sauce over the pasta, then top with the ricotta.

Preparation time 15 minutes • **Total time** 35 minutes • **Per serving** 387 calories, 6.9 g. fat (16% of calories), 2.2 g. saturated fat, 42 mg. cholesterol, 110 mg. sodium, 3.2 g. dietary fiber, 184 mg. calcium, 5 mg. iron, 35 mg. vitamin C, 1 mg. beta-carotene • **Serves 4**

FOOD FACTS
Black and red pepper, despite their common name, come from different plants. Black pepper is the dried, unripe berries ("peppercorns") of the *Piper nigrum* vine, while red pepper flakes are dried, crushed chili peppers, which, like bell peppers, belong to the *Capsicum* family.

ON THE MENU
Serve a tricolor salad made with Belgian endive, arugula and radicchio.

SPICY CHICKEN AND PASTA SALAD

½ **cup defatted reduced-sodium chicken broth**

6 **ounces boneless, skinless chicken breast halves, cut crosswise into ½-inch-thick strips**

8 **ounces gemelli or fusilli pasta**

2 **cups small broccoli florets**

1 **cup carrot sticks**

1 **cup snow peas**

¼ **cup loosely packed Italian parsley sprigs**

2 **scallions, cut up**

1 **fresh jalapeño pepper, halved, seeded and cut into chunks**

3 **tablespoons reduced-fat mayonnaise**

2 **tablespoons nonfat sour cream**

1 **tablespoon fresh lemon juice**

The pasta called *gemelli* is made up of two short strands twisted together at one end—hence the name, which means "twins." You may not find gemelli in your supermarket, but fusilli or rotini would provide an equally good foil for the creamy, chili-laced dressing, strips of chicken and crisp-tender vegetables.

1 Bring a large covered pot of water to a boil over high heat.

2 Meanwhile, bring the broth to a boil in a covered medium skillet over high heat. Stir in the chicken strips, return to a boil and reduce the heat to low; cover and simmer, turning occasionally, for 3 to 4 minutes, or until the chicken is cooked through. With a slotted spoon, transfer the chicken to a plate; cover chicken loosely with foil. Increase the heat to high and boil the broth for 3 to 5 minutes, or until reduced to a syrupy consistency. Remove the pan from the heat.

3 While the broth is cooking down, add the pasta to the boiling water and return to a boil; cook for 8 to 10 minutes or according to package directions until al dente. About 4 minutes before the pasta is done, add the broccoli and carrots. One minute before the pasta is done, add the snow peas. Cook until the vegetables are crisp-tender and the pasta is done. Drain in a colander and cool under cold running water; drain again. Transfer the pasta and vegetables to a salad bowl.

4 Combine the parsley, scallions, jalapeño, mayonnaise, sour cream, lemon juice and the reduced broth in a food processor, and process until puréed.

5 Pour the dressing over the salad, add the chicken and toss to mix.

To string a snow-pea pod, pinch the stem end with your fingers, then pull downward on the string.

Preparation time 20 minutes • **Total time** 35 minutes • **Per serving** 348 calories, 4.9 g. fat (13% of calories), 1 g. saturated fat, 28 mg. cholesterol, 207 mg. sodium, 5.8 g. dietary fiber, 87 mg. calcium, 4 mg. iron, 88 mg. vitamin C, 5.5 mg. beta-carotene • **Serves 4**

❦ ❦ ❦

TURKEY-MACARONI CASSEROLE

- 8 ounces macaroni, such as elbows
- 4 ounces fresh mushrooms, sliced
- 3 tablespoons defatted chicken broth
- 8 ounces part-skim ricotta cheese
- 2 ounces shredded part-skim mozzarella cheese
- 2 large egg whites
- 2 tablespoons grated Parmesan cheese
- 2 tablespoons skim milk
- ¼ teaspoon freshly ground black pepper
- 4 ounces skinless roast turkey breast, diced
- ½ cup coarsely chopped fresh basil leaves
- 1 can (8 ounces) no-salt-added tomato sauce

Macaroni-with-meat casseroles have a long history in America, and these days they are often made with a packaged mix. But for flavor and nutrition, nothing beats a homemade noodle bake put together from fresh ingredients.

1 Preheat the oven to 375°. Spray an 11 x 7-inch baking dish with no-stick spray.

2 Bring a large covered pot of water to a boil over high heat. Add the pasta to the boiling water, return to a boil and cook for 6 to 7 minutes or according to package directions until al dente. Drain in a colander, rinse briefly under cold running water and drain again.

3 While the pasta is cooking, combine the mushrooms and broth in a large no-stick skillet. Bring the broth to a boil over high heat and sauté for 4 to 6 minutes, or until the mushrooms are tender. Remove the skillet from the heat.

4 In a large bowl combine the ricotta, mozzarella, egg whites, Parmesan, milk and pepper; beat together with a wooden spoon until well blended. Stir in the mushrooms and their broth, the turkey and basil, then add the drained pasta. Spoon the mixture into the prepared baking dish.

5 Pour the tomato sauce over the pasta mixture and bake for 20 to 25 minutes, or until hot and bubbly.

Preparation time 15 minutes • **Total time** 55 minutes • **Per serving** 421 calories, 9.3 g. fat (20% of calories), 4.9 g. saturated fat, 51 mg. cholesterol, 294 mg. sodium, 2.6 g. dietary fiber, 354 mg. calcium, 5 mg. iron, 11 mg. vitamin C, 0.6 mg. beta-carotene • **Serves 4**

Using skinless turkey breast instead of beef in this casserole keeps the fat content healthfully low.

FOOD FACT

Ricotta cheese was originally made by cooking the whey drained off during the production of other types of cheese. Today, this versatile cheese is made by combining whey with whole or skim milk.

KITCHEN TIPS

Many foods, like the mushrooms in this recipe, can be sautéed without fat, using broth, wine, juice or even water instead of oil or butter. A no-stick pan is an asset when you use this fat-cutting technique.

PASTA CAESAR SALAD WITH CHICKEN

3 tablespoons nonfat mayonnaise

1 ounce Parmesan cheese, coarsely grated

2 tablespoons Italian parsley sprigs

1 tablespoon plus 1 teaspoon fresh lemon juice

1 tablespoon defatted reduced-sodium chicken broth

2 garlic cloves, crushed

1 teaspoon anchovy paste

½ teaspoon freshly ground black pepper

6 ounces cavatappi pasta

8 ounces thin-sliced chicken cutlets, cut into 1-inch pieces

⅛ teaspoon salt

1 bunch arugula or watercress, washed, tough stems removed

Caesar salad is said to have been created in the 1920s by chef Caesar Cardini, owner of a restaurant in Tijuana, Mexico. The greens, garlicky dressing and a lightly cooked egg are often tossed together with a flourish at tableside. For this variation, Caesar dressing, flavored with anchovy paste and Parmesan, is tossed with pasta, tart greens and morsels of broiled chicken.

1 Bring a large covered pot of water to a boil over high heat. Preheat the broiler. Spray a jelly-roll pan with no-stick spray.

2 Meanwhile, combine the mayonnaise, 1 tablespoon of the Parmesan, the parsley sprigs, 1 tablespoon of the lemon juice, the broth, half of the garlic, the anchovy paste and ¼ teaspoon of the pepper in a food processor or blender, and process until smooth.

3 Add the pasta to the boiling water, return to a boil and cook for 8 to 10 minutes or according to package directions until al dente. Drain in a colander and cool briefly under cold running water; drain again.

4 Place the chicken in the prepared pan. Drizzle the remaining 1 teaspoon lemon juice over the chicken. Sprinkle with the remaining crushed garlic, the remaining ¼ teaspoon pepper and the salt, and toss to mix. Broil 3 to 4 inches from the heat for 3 to 5 minutes, or until the chicken is cooked through and lightly browned. Remove from the heat.

5 Transfer the pasta to a salad bowl. Add the arugula or watercress, the dressing, the chicken and any juices that have collected in the pan, and the remaining Parmesan. Toss to coat well.

Preparation time 15 minutes • **Total time** 30 minutes • **Per serving** 274 calories, 3.9 g. fat (13% of calories), 1.7 g. saturated fat, 39 mg. cholesterol, 394 mg. sodium, 2.1 g. dietary fiber, 172 mg. calcium, 2 mg. iron, 23 mg. vitamin C, 1.3 mg. beta-carotene • **Serves 4**

❧ ❧ ❧

GARLICKY SPAGHETTI WITH TURKEY

8 **ounces perciatelli or spaghetti**

8 **ounces green beans, trimmed and cut in half**

1 **tablespoon plus 1 teaspoon extra-virgin olive oil**

½ **teaspoon crushed red pepper flakes**

3 **garlic cloves, crushed**

6 **ounces julienne-cut skinless roast turkey breast**

¾ **cup julienne-cut roasted red peppers (freshly roasted or from a jar)**

1 **tablespoon cider vinegar**

¼ **teaspoon salt**

Store-bought roasted peppers are a convenience, but nothing rivals the flavor of freshly roasted bell peppers. The method shown below is simple and quick, using quartered, stemmed and seeded peppers rather than whole ones.

1 Bring a large covered pot of water to a boil over high heat.

2 Add the pasta to the boiling water, return to a boil and cook for 10 to 12 minutes or according to package directions until al dente. About 5 minutes before the pasta is cooked, add the beans and cook until the pasta is al dente and the beans are crisp-tender. Drain in a colander and transfer to a large serving bowl.

3 In a small skillet, stir together the oil and pepper flakes. Place over medium heat and cook, stirring constantly, for 2 minutes. Stir in the garlic and cook, stirring constantly, for 30 seconds, or until fragrant. Immediately pour the hot oil mixture over the pasta and beans.

4 Add the turkey, red peppers, vinegar and salt to the pasta mixture, and toss to combine.

Preparation time 10 minutes • **Total time** 30 minutes • **Per serving** 350 calories, 7.7 g. fat (20% of calories), 1.5 g. saturated fat, 33 mg. cholesterol, 179 mg. sodium, 2.3 g. dietary fiber, 47 mg. calcium, 4 mg. iron, 40 mg. vitamin C, 0.8 mg. beta-carotene • **Serves 4**

Arrange quartered, stemmed, seeded peppers, skin-side up, on a foil-lined baking pan. Broil until well charred.

Place the roasted peppers in a bowl and cover it. Let the peppers steam for a few minutes to loosen their skins.

Scrape off the charred skin with a table knife. If neccessary, rub off stubborn patches of char under cold running water.

Pasta with Meat

❧ ❧ ❧

OLD AND NEW FAVORITES—FROM
CHUNKY SAUCE TO SATISFYING SALAD—
MADE WITH THE LEANEST CUTS OF
BEEF, VEAL, PORK AND LAMB

PASTA WITH SWEET PEPPERS AND HAM

1½ teaspoons extra-virgin olive oil

2 large red bell peppers, coarsely diced

1 large onion, coarsely diced

4 garlic cloves, minced

½ teaspoon dried oregano, crumbled

¼ teaspoon crushed red pepper flakes

3 ounces boiled ham, diced

½ cup defatted low-sodium chicken broth

8 ounces penne rigate (ribbed penne) or regular penne pasta

1 ounce Parmesan cheese, coarsely grated

¼ cup chopped fresh Italian parsley

⅛ teaspoon freshly ground black pepper

A shaker of domestic grated Parmesan is handy for hurry-up meals, but its flavor cannot rival that of freshly grated Italian cheese. Domestic Parmesan, aged for as little as 10 months, is a firm, mild cheese, while the best imported Parmesan, designated "Parmigiano Reggiano," is aged for at least two years to develop a well-rounded, sharp-sweet flavor and a granular texture. With a good Parmesan cheese, you can use less and still enjoy a full flavor.

1 Bring a large covered pot of water to a boil over high heat.

2 Meanwhile, in a medium saucepan over high heat, warm the oil until very hot but not smoking. Add the bell peppers, onions, garlic, oregano and red pepper flakes. Sauté, stirring, for 2 to 3 minutes, or until the vegetables begin to soften and release their juices. Stir in the ham, then add 3 tablespoons of the broth and bring to a simmer. Reduce the heat to medium, cover and simmer, stirring occasionally, for 8 to 9 minutes, or until the vegetables are very tender. (If the pan gets too dry, add an additional tablespoon of broth.)

3 Meanwhile, add the pasta to the boiling water, return to a boil and cook for 10 to 12 minutes or according to package directions until al dente. Reserving ½ cup of the pasta cooking liquid, drain the pasta in a colander and transfer to a warmed serving bowl.

4 Add the remaining broth and the reserved pasta cooking liquid to the vegetable mixture. Increase the heat to high, bring to a boil and simmer for 3 minutes to reduce the liquid slightly.

5 Pour the sauce over the pasta. Add the Parmesan, parsley and black pepper, and toss to coat well.

Preparation time 15 minutes • **Total time** 45 minutes • **Per serving** 348 calories, 7.1 g. fat (18% of calories), 2.5 g. saturated fat, 18 mg. cholesterol, 467 mg. sodium, 3.6 g. dietary fiber, 141 mg. calcium, 4 mg. iron, 155 mg. vitamin C, 2.7 mg. beta-carotene • **Serves 4**

A French rotary grater with interchangeable drums can produce fine or coarse shreds or chips of cheese, nuts or chocolate.

Preceding pages: Radiatore with Mexican Pork Stew (recipe on page 61).

BOW-TIES WITH CURRIED BEEF

1 cup plain nonfat yogurt

8 ounces lean, trimmed boneless beef sirloin or top round steak

2 garlic cloves, crushed

1½ teaspoons curry powder

1½ teaspoons ground cumin

6 ounces bow-tie pasta

⅓ cup defatted chicken broth

¼ cup water

1½ cups small cauliflower florets

1½ cups snow peas

¼ cup chopped fresh cilantro

¼ teaspoon salt

Pinch of ground red pepper

Yogurt-cheese funnels are made of fine plastic mesh. Stand the funnel over a bowl or cup and spoon in the yogurt; place in the refrigerator until the yogurt is as thick as you like.

Yogurt, when briefly drained, gets as thick as sour cream, providing a low-fat base for creamy sauces. If you use drained yogurt often (it can substitute for heavy cream or cream cheese, too), buy an inexpensive yogurt funnel like the one shown.

1 Line a coffee-filter cone with a paper filter (or line a small strainer with a white paper towel) and place over a small bowl. Spoon the yogurt into the filter or strainer and let drain for 15 minutes.

2 While the yogurt drains, bring a large covered pot of water to a boil over high heat. Meanwhile, preheat the broiler and the broiler pan and rack. Rub the steak with the garlic, ½ teaspoon of the curry powder and ½ teaspoon of the cumin. Let stand for 5 minutes.

3 Place the steak on the broiler-pan rack and broil 4 to 6 inches from the heat source for 5 minutes per side, or until medium-rare. Transfer to a plate and let stand for 5 minutes.

4 While the steak broils, add the pasta to the boiling water, return to a boil and cook for 10 to 12 minutes or according to package directions until al dente. Drain in a colander and transfer to a serving bowl.

5 In a medium skillet, bring the broth and water to a boil over high heat. Add the cauliflower, reduce the heat to medium-high, cover and cook for 3 to 4 minutes, or until crisp-tender. Uncover the pan, stir in the snow peas and cook for 1 to 2 minutes longer, or until crisp-tender. Pour the vegetable mixture over the pasta.

6 Mix the drained yogurt with the cilantro, the remaining 1 teaspoon curry powder, remaining 1 teaspoon cumin and the salt and red pepper. Add the yogurt mixture to the pasta and toss to coat.

7 Transfer the steak to a cutting board; pour any juices from the plate over the pasta. Thinly slice the steak, add it to the pasta and toss.

Preparation time 10 minutes • **Total time** 35 minutes • **Per serving** 314 calories, 4.4 g. fat (12% of calories), 1.4 g. saturated fat, 39 mg. cholesterol, 301 mg. sodium, 3.6 g. dietary fiber, 175 mg. calcium, 5 mg. iron, 60 mg. vitamin C, 0.1 mg. beta-carotene • **Serves 4**

Pasta with Veal and Lemon

1 tablespoon plus 1 teaspoon extra-virgin olive oil

1½ cups thinly sliced shallots

1 teaspoon granulated sugar

2 teaspoons grated lemon zest

1½ cups defatted chicken broth

1 cup julienne-cut carrots

8 ounces tricolor fusilli

8 ounces veal scaloppine, cut into ½-inch-wide strips

¼ teaspoon freshly ground black pepper

1 tablespoon all-purpose flour

1 tablespoon fresh lemon juice

1 tablespoon cornstarch dissolved in 1 tablespoon cold water

1 ripe medium tomato, diced

Here is a light dish based on veal piccata. Shallots, rather than the traditional garlic, are used in this recipe; to save peeling time, choose large-cloved shallots.

1 Bring a large covered pot of water to a boil over high heat.

2 Meanwhile, in a heavy, medium skillet, warm 1 teaspoon of the oil over medium-high heat. Add the shallots, sprinkle with the sugar and 1 teaspoon of the lemon zest, and stir well; reduce the heat to medium-low. Drizzle in 1 tablespoon of the broth and cook, stirring frequently, for about 12 minutes, or until the shallots are lightly browned and very tender. (Add up to ⅓ cup more broth as necessary.)

3 Stir in the carrots and add ¼ cup more broth; increase the heat to medium-high and bring to a boil. Cover and simmer, stirring once or twice, for 3 to 4 minutes, or until the carrots are just tender. Remove the skillet from the heat and set aside.

4 Add the pasta to the boiling water and return to a boil. Cook for 9 to 11 minutes or according to package directions until al dente. Drain the pasta in a colander, then transfer it to a serving bowl.

5 Toss the veal with the remaining 1 teaspoon lemon zest and the pepper, then with the flour. In a large no-stick skillet heat the remaining 1 tablespoon oil over high heat. Add the veal and sauté for 2 to 3 minutes, or until just cooked through. Transfer the veal to a plate.

6 Add the remaining broth and the lemon juice to the no-stick skillet; cook over high heat for 3 minutes, stirring to get up any browned bits from the bottom of the pan. Stir in the cornstarch mixture and bring to a boil, stirring constantly. Stir in the tomatoes and cook, stirring frequently, for 2 minutes, or until the tomatoes just start to soften. Add the shallot mixture, the veal and any juices that have collected on the plate, and heat through. Pour over the pasta and toss to mix.

Preparation time 20 minutes • **Total time** 45 minutes • **Per serving** 404 calories, 7 g. fat (16% of calories), 1.1 g. saturated fat, 44 mg. cholesterol, 452 mg. sodium, 4.5 g. dietary fiber, 60 mg. calcium, 4 mg. iron, 19 mg. vitamin C, 4.9 mg. beta-carotene
Serves 4

GREEK-STYLE PASTA WITH MEAT

- 6 ounces lean, trimmed boneless leg of lamb or beef top round, cut into chunks
- 2 teaspoons olive oil
- 1 large onion, chopped
- 3 garlic cloves, minced
- ¼ teaspoon dried oregano
- ¼ teaspoon dried thyme
- ¼ teaspoon dried mint
- ¼ teaspoon freshly ground black pepper
- Large pinch of ground cinnamon
- 1 can (16 ounces) crushed tomatoes in purée
- 1 can (8 ounces) no-salt-added tomato sauce
- 10 ounces orzo pasta
- 1 ounce feta cheese, crumbled

The pasta most associated with Greece is one shaped like grains of rice. In the United States, it is usually sold as *orzo*, which is the Italian word for barley. Most small pasta shapes—orzo, ring-shaped *anellini*, thimble-shaped *ditalini* and the tiny "butter-flies" called *farfalline*, for example—are used in soup, but *orzo* is often served like rice. Here, it is the base for a meat sauce seasoned with the distinctively Greek combination of oregano and cinnamon.

1 Bring a large covered pot of water to a boil over high heat.

2 Process the lamb or beef in a food processor just until ground.

3 Warm the oil in a large, heavy skillet over medium-high heat. Add the onions and garlic, and sauté for 3 to 5 minutes, or until the onions are tender and lightly browned. Crumble in the ground meat and cook, stirring, for 2 to 3 minutes, or until it is no longer pink; add a tablespoon of water if the pan gets too dry. Stir in the oregano, thyme, mint, pepper and cinnamon; cook, stirring constantly, for 30 seconds.

4 Stir in the crushed tomatoes and tomato sauce and bring to a boil. Reduce the heat to low and simmer, stirring occasionally, for 10 minutes, or until the flavors are blended.

5 While the sauce simmers, add the pasta to the boiling water, return to a boil and cook for 6 to 8 minutes or according to package directions until al dente. Drain in a colander and transfer to a warmed serving bowl.

6 Spoon the meat sauce over the pasta and sprinkle with the feta.

Feta cheese is packed in brine. Rinse the cheese in cold water before using if you find it too salty or if you're trying to cut down on your intake of sodium.

Preparation time 15 minutes • **Total time** 40 minutes • **Per serving** 432 calories, 7.1 g. fat (15% of calories), 2.2 g. saturated fat, 34 mg. cholesterol, 305 mg. sodium, 3.5 g. dietary fiber, 110 mg. calcium, 5 mg. iron, 31 mg. vitamin C, 0.9 mg. beta-carotene • **Serves 4**

RADIATORE WITH MEXICAN PORK STEW

6 ounces lean, boneless loin pork chops, cut into ½-inch cubes

3 teaspoons chili powder

2 teaspoons olive oil

1 large green bell pepper, finely diced

1 large onion, minced

1 can (4 ounces) chopped green chilies, rinsed and drained

3 garlic cloves, minced

1 teaspoon ground cumin

½ teaspoon dried oregano, crumbled

⅛ teaspoon salt

1 can (10½ ounces) red kidney beans, rinsed and drained

1 cup defatted reduced-sodium chicken broth

6 ounces radiatore pasta

1 cup frozen corn kernels

¼ cup chopped fresh cilantro or 2 tablespoons chopped fresh Italian parsley

This dish was inspired by Mexican *posole*, which is made with hominy (hulled corn). Here, corn kernels stand in for hominy, but the other ingredients—bell pepper, onion, chilies, garlic, cumin and oregano—are traditional. To tenderize the pork, pound the chops lightly, using a rolling pin or meat mallet.

1 Bring a large covered pot of water to a boil over high heat.

2 Meanwhile, place the pork cubes on a sheet of wax paper; sprinkle with 1 teaspoon of the chili powder and toss to coat. Let stand for 5 minutes.

3 In a large, heavy saucepan, warm the oil over high heat until hot but not smoking. Add the pork and sauté for 1 to 2 minutes, or until lightly browned. Using a slotted spoon, transfer the pork to a plate.

4 Add the bell peppers, onions, chilies, garlic, cumin, oregano, salt and the remaining 2 teaspoons chili powder to the pan. Sauté for 2 to 3 minutes, or until the vegetables start to soften. Add the beans and broth, and bring to a boil. Reduce the heat to low, cover and simmer, stirring occasionally, for 10 minutes, or until the vegetables are tender.

5 While the stew is cooking, add the pasta to the boiling water, return to a boil and cook for 10 to 12 minutes or according to package directions until al dente. Drain the pasta in a colander and transfer to a warmed serving bowl.

6 Remove 1 cup of the stew and purée in a food processor or blender. Stir the purée back into the pan, then add the corn and pork, along with any juices that have accumulated on the plate. Increase the heat to medium and simmer the stew, uncovered, for 5 minutes.

7 Remove the pan from the heat and stir in the cilantro or parsley. Pour the stew over the pasta and toss to mix.

Preparation time 17 minutes • **Total time** 45 minutes • **Per serving** 379 calories, 6.7 g. fat (16% of calories), 1.2 g. saturated fat, 27 mg. cholesterol, 550 mg. sodium, 7.1 g. dietary fiber, 69 mg. calcium, 4 mg. iron, 51 mg. vitamin C, 0.7 mg. beta-carotene • **Serves 4**

TORTELLONI WITH VEGETABLE SAUCE

2 cans (14½ ounces each) no-salt-added stewed tomatoes with their juice

2 tablespoons no-salt-added tomato paste

1 medium zucchini, thinly sliced

1 medium yellow squash, thinly sliced

2 garlic cloves, crushed

2 teaspoons dried Italian herb seasoning (see page 13)

12 ounces fresh or frozen meat tortelloni

2 teaspoons cornstarch

2 tablespoons grated Parmesan cheese

¼ cup chopped fresh basil, or 2 tablespoons chopped Italian parsley

Filled pastas such as tortelloni and the smaller tortellini are sold both fresh and frozen in many supermarkets. They are almost a meal in themselves, requiring just a simple sauce and a salad to make a well-balanced dinner. This sauce, made with tomatoes and summer squash, can also be served over unfilled pasta such as rotelle.

1 Bring a large covered pot of water to a boil over high heat.

2 Meanwhile, in a cup, set aside 1 tablespoon of the juice from the stewed tomatoes. In a large, heavy saucepan, stir together the stewed tomatoes with their remaining juice and the tomato paste. Stir in the zucchini, yellow squash, garlic and Italian seasoning; cover and bring to a boil over medium-high heat. Reduce the heat to low; simmer, stirring occasionally, for 5 minutes, or until the vegetables are tender.

3 Add the pasta to the boiling water, return to a boil and cook for 8 to 10 minutes or according to package directions until al dente. Drain the pasta in a colander and transfer to a warmed serving bowl.

4 Stir the cornstarch into the reserved tomato juice. Stir the cornstarch mixture and the Parmesan into the vegetable sauce and bring to a boil, stirring constantly; the sauce will thicken slightly. Remove the pan from the heat and stir in the basil or parsley.

5 Pour the vegetable sauce over the pasta and serve.

Preparation time 11 minutes • **Total time** 25 minutes • **Per serving** 355 calories, 5.4 g. fat (14% of calories), 0.7 g. saturated fat, 52 mg. cholesterol, 496 mg. sodium, 5.8 g. dietary fiber, 224 mg. calcium, 5 mg. iron, 40 mg. vitamin C, 1.1 mg. beta-carotene • **Serves 4**

ON THE MENU
Try an Italian salad of thinly sliced fennel, sliced mushrooms (either nut-brown cremini or white button mushrooms) and shavings of Parmesan, lightly dressed with a lemon vinaigrette.

FOR A CHANGE
There are lots of stuffed pastas, with a variety of fillings, to sample: *cappelletti* (little hats), the filled pasta crescents called *agnolotti* and triangular *pansotti* as well as the more familiar tortellini and ravioli.

PENNE AND STEAK SALAD

½ cup (1 ounce) sun-dried tomatoes (not packed in oil)

1 cup water

6 ounces penne pasta

8 ounces lean, trimmed boneless beef sirloin or top round steak

2 garlic cloves, crushed

½ teaspoon coarsely cracked black pepper

2 tablespoons defatted beef broth

1 tablespoon fresh lemon juice

2 teaspoons reduced-sodium soy sauce

1½ teaspoons grated fresh ginger

1 teaspoon Dijon mustard

1 teaspoon extra-virgin olive oil

1 bunch watercress, washed, tough stems removed

1 cup thinly sliced kirby or English cucumbers

Hearty and light at the same time, warm salads are welcome in any weather. This one has a lovely balance of crisp and tender textures, spicy and fresh flavors, and a vibrant red-white-and-green color scheme: Slices of juicy garlic-rubbed steak are combined with penne, sun-dried tomatoes, watercress and cucumbers, and tossed with a soy-ginger-mustard dressing.

1 Bring a large covered pot of water to a boil over high heat. Preheat the broiler and a broiler pan and rack.

2 Put the dried tomatoes and water in a small saucepan and bring to a boil over high heat. Remove the pan from the heat, cover and let stand for 5 minutes, or until the tomatoes have softened. Drain the tomatoes in a small strainer, then rinse under cold running water until cool. Cut the tomatoes into small pieces.

3 Add the pasta to the boiling water, return to a boil and cook for 10 to 12 minutes or according to package directions until al dente. Drain in a colander and rinse briefly under cold running water; drain again.

4 Rub the steak with half of the garlic and all of the pepper. Place the steak on the broiler-pan rack and broil 4 to 6 inches from the heat for 5 minutes per side, or until medium-rare. Transfer the steak to a plate and let stand for 5 minutes while you make the dressing.

5 In a salad bowl, whisk together the broth, lemon juice, soy sauce, ginger, mustard, oil and the remaining garlic.

6 Transfer the steak to a cutting board. Add any juices that have collected on the plate to the salad dressing. Carve the steak into thin slices.

7 Add the pasta, dried tomatoes, watercress, cucumbers and steak to the salad bowl, and toss to mix.

Soak the sun-dried tomatoes in boiling water for a few minutes to soften them, then rinse and drain the tomatoes before cutting them up.

Preparation time 15 minutes • **Total time** 35 minutes • **Per serving** 290 calories, 5.3 g. fat (17% of calories), 1.5 g. saturated fat, 38 mg. cholesterol, 223 mg. sodium, 3.9 g. dietary fiber, 80 mg. calcium, 4 mg. iron, 43 mg. vitamin C, 2 mg. beta-carotene
Serves 4

WARM PASTA ANTIPASTO SALAD

- 6 ounces bow-tie pasta
- 2 teaspoons extra-virgin olive oil
- 1 large red bell pepper, quartered, then cut crosswise into thin slices
- 1 medium red onion, thinly sliced
- 2 garlic cloves, minced
- ½ teaspoon freshly ground black pepper
- ¼ teaspoon dried Italian herb seasoning, crumbled (see page 13)
- ⅛ teaspoon salt
- 1 small zucchini, thinly sliced
- 2 tablespoons defatted reduced-sodium chicken broth
- 2 tablespoons water
- 2 cups halved cherry tomatoes
- 1 can (10½ ounces) cannellini beans, rinsed and drained
- 2 ounces sliced provolone cheese, cut into strips
- 2 ounces thinly sliced ham, cut into strips
- 1 tablespoon red wine vinegar
- 6 kalamata or ripe olives, sliced off pits

A s you enter a fine Italian restaurant, you'll pass a table laden with a mouth-watering array of *antipasti*—roasted peppers, olives, marinated vegetables and beans, cheeses, smoked meats and chilled seafood—that serve to sharpen the appetite for the meal to come. This bountiful salad combines the *antipasti* with the pasta course. As a time-saver, the sauce is started before the pasta is done.

1 Bring a large covered pot of water to a boil over high heat.

2 Add the pasta to the boiling water, return to a boil and cook, stirring frequently, for 10 to 12 minutes or according to package directions until al dente. Drain in a colander and cool under cold running water until the pasta is just warm.

3 While the pasta is cooking, in a large, deep skillet, warm the oil over high heat. Add the bell peppers, onions, garlic, black pepper, Italian seasoning and salt, and sauté for 3 to 4 minutes, or until the bell peppers are crisp-tender. Stir in the zucchini, broth and water, and bring to a boil. Reduce the heat to medium, cover and cook, stirring occasionally, for 3 to 4 minutes, or until the zucchini is tender. Add the tomatoes and toss gently to mix; cover and cook for 1 minute longer, or until the tomatoes are just heated but not cooked. Transfer the vegetable mixture to a serving bowl.

4 Add the drained pasta, beans, cheese, ham, vinegar and olives to the bowl, and toss to mix.

Preparation time 20 minutes • **Total time** 40 minutes • **Per serving** 358 calories, 9.6 g. fat (24% of calories), 3.5 g. saturated fat, 18 mg. cholesterol, 558 mg. sodium, 6.2 g. dietary fiber, 166 mg. calcium, 4 mg. iron, 71 mg. vitamin C, 1.2 mg. beta-carotene • **Serves 4**

❧   ❧   ❧

MAKE-AHEAD
You can make the salad in advance and serve it chilled or at room temperature.

FOOD FACT
Firm, golden, smoky-flavored provolone cheese is a specialty of southern Italy.

Provolone melts beautifully and is excellent for sandwiches and casseroles.

ON THE MENU
End the meal with oranges—peeled, sliced crosswise, sprinkled with cinnamon and a pinch of sugar, and thoroughly chilled.

PASTA WITH LAMB AND ROSEMARY PESTO

1 large lemon

6 ounces spinach, washed, tough stems removed

3 tablespoons defatted beef broth

½ teaspoon dried rosemary leaves

¼ teaspoon freshly ground black pepper

¼ teaspoon salt

⅛ teaspoon crushed red pepper flakes

1 garlic clove, peeled

8 ounces lean, trimmed, boneless lamb steak

8 ounces long fusilli or fettuccine

3 large carrots, halved lengthwise and cut into long diagonal slices

1 tablespoon grated Parmesan cheese

Use a small rubber spatula—or your hands—to spread the rosemary pesto over the lamb steak.

Pesto *alla Genovese*, known to every lover of Italian food, is made from basil, garlic, olive oil, Parmesan and pine nuts. Here is a very different pesto, composed of spinach, rosemary, garlic and lemon juice. The fragrant herb mixture is rubbed on lamb steak before it's broiled and is also tossed with the pasta.

1 Bring a large covered pot of water to a boil over high heat.

2 Meanwhile, with a swivel-bladed vegetable peeler, remove a 2-inch strip of zest from the lemon. Squeeze 2 tablespoons of juice from the lemon. Combine the lemon juice, spinach, broth, rosemary, black pepper, salt and crushed red pepper in a food processor. With the machine running, drop the lemon zest and the garlic through the feed tube and process until puréed.

3 Preheat the broiler, broiler pan and broiler rack. Place the lamb steak on a plate and spread 2 tablespoons of the rosemary pesto over it, coating both sides. Let stand for 5 minutes.

4 Place the lamb on the broiler-pan rack and broil 4 to 5 inches from the heat source for 4 to 5 minutes per side for medium-rare. Transfer to a clean plate and let stand for 5 minutes.

5 While the lamb broils, add the pasta to the boiling water, return to a boil and cook for 8 to 10 minutes or according to package directions until al dente. Three minutes before the pasta is done, add the carrots and cook until tender. Drain the pasta and carrots in a colander and transfer to a heated serving bowl. Toss the pasta and carrots with the remaining pesto.

6 Transfer the lamb to a cutting board. Pour any juices that have collected on the plate into the pasta. Carve the lamb into thin slices, place on top of the pasta and toss gently, then sprinkle with the Parmesan.

Preparation time 10 minutes • **Total time** 35 minutes • **Per serving** 351 calories, 6.1 g. fat (16% of calories), 2.1 g. saturated fat, 41 mg. cholesterol, 292 mg. sodium, 4.6 g. dietary fiber, 97 mg. calcium, 4 mg. iron, 20 mg. vitamin C, 14 mg. beta-carotene • **Serves 4**

THAI NOODLES WITH BEEF AND BASIL

8 ounces lean beef top round, cut into chunks

3 garlic cloves, crushed

1 tablespoon reduced-sodium soy sauce

1 teaspoon anchovy paste

1 teaspoon dried mint

½ teaspoon granulated sugar

¼ teaspoon crushed red pepper flakes

2½ teaspoons olive oil

1 large red bell pepper, halved and thinly sliced crosswise

1 medium red onion, thinly sliced

¼ cup defatted reduced-sodium beef broth

2 large tomatoes, coarsely chopped in a food processor or by hand

1 tablespoon plus 2 teaspoons fresh lime juice

8 ounces medium-thin egg noodles

½ cup coarsely chopped fresh basil

Rather than using the saltshaker, Thai cooks season most of their savory dishes with a few drops of *nam pla*, an intensely aromatic sauce made by fermenting a mixture of fresh anchovies and salt for a year or longer. Although Thai food is becoming more popular each year, *nam pla* is not yet widely available; here, a combination of soy sauce and anchovy paste takes its place.

1 Bring a large covered pot of water to a boil over high heat.

2 Meanwhile, place the beef chunks in a food processor and process until finely ground. Add the garlic, soy sauce, anchovy paste, mint, sugar and red pepper flakes, and pulse just until blended.

3 In a large, deep no-stick skillet, warm 2 teaspoons of the oil over high heat until hot but not smoking. Add the bell peppers and onions, and sauté for 5 minutes, or until the vegetables are crisp-tender. (If the pan gets too dry, add a little of the broth.)

4 Crumble in the beef mixture; drizzle with 2 tablespoons of the broth and sauté for 2 to 3 minutes, or until the meat is no longer pink. Add the remaining 2 tablespoons broth, the tomatoes and lime juice, and toss to blend well. Bring to a boil, reduce the heat to low, cover and simmer, stirring occasionally, for 5 minutes, or until the flavors are blended.

5 Meanwhile, add the noodles to the boiling water, return to a boil and cook for 6 to 8 minutes or according to package directions until al dente. Drain in a colander and transfer to a large warmed serving bowl. Toss the noodles with the remaining ½ teaspoon olive oil to prevent sticking.

6 Pour the beef mixture over the noodles, then add the basil and toss gently to mix.

Preparation time 25 minutes • **Total time** 45 minutes • **Per serving** 372 calories, 7.6 g. fat (18% of calories), 1.6 g. saturated fat, 87 mg. cholesterol, 290 mg. sodium, 3.6 g. dietary fiber, 94 mg. calcium, 6 mg. iron, 71 mg. vitamin C, 1.3 mg. beta-carotene • **Serves 4**

Pasta with Vegetables

❧ ❧ ❧

THE BEST OF THE GARDEN'S
SEASONAL BOUNTY, PARTNERED
WITH PASTA, MAKES QUICK,
COLORFUL MEALS

CHILI BEAN PASTA

1 tablespoon plus 1 teaspoon olive oil

1 large onion, chopped

1 large red bell pepper, diced

1 can (4 ounces) chopped green chilies, rinsed and drained

3 garlic cloves, minced

1 large fresh jalapeño pepper, partially seeded and diced

1¼ teaspoons ground cumin

¼ teaspoon freshly ground pepper

1 can (16 ounces) crushed tomatoes in purée

1 can (10½ ounces) black beans, rinsed and drained

1 can (8 ounces) no-salt-added tomato sauce

2 tablespoons water

8 ounces fusilli pasta

¼ cup chopped fresh cilantro or 2 tablespoons chopped fresh Italian parsley

Much of the heat in chili peppers lies in their seeds and ribs, so you can fine-tune the hotness of a dish by including more or less of these potent parts of the jalapeño. Wear thin rubber or plastic gloves when preparing hot chilies, and don't touch your mouth, nose and especially your eyes when working with them. If you choose not to wear gloves, wash your hands thoroughly with soap and water, and even after you do so, avoid touching your eyes.

1 Bring a large covered pot of water to a boil over high heat.

2 Meanwhile, warm the oil in a large, deep skillet over high heat. Add the onions, bell peppers, green chilies, garlic and jalapeños, and stir to coat with the oil. Reduce the heat to medium-high and cook, stirring frequently, for 3 to 5 minutes, or until the vegetables are tender. Add the cumin and ground pepper; cook, stirring, for 30 seconds.

3 Add the crushed tomatoes, beans, tomato sauce and water to the vegetables, and bring to a boil. Reduce the heat to low, cover and simmer, stirring occasionally, for 15 minutes, or until the flavors are blended. Uncover, increase the heat to medium and simmer for 5 minutes longer.

4 While the sauce simmers, add the pasta to the boiling water. Return to a boil and cook for 10 to 12 minutes or according to package directions until al dente. Drain in a colander and transfer to a warmed serving bowl.

5 Pour the sauce over the pasta, sprinkle with the cilantro or parsley and toss to mix well.

Preparation time 12 minutes • **Total time** 45 minutes • **Per serving** 389 calories, 6.3 g. fat (14% of calories), 0.8 g. saturated fat, 0 mg. cholesterol, 494 mg. sodium, 6.2 g. dietary fiber, 95 mg. calcium, 5 mg. iron, 135 mg. vitamin C, 2.3 mg. beta-carotene • **Serves 4**

Preceding pages: Shells with Double-Mushroom Sauce (recipe on page 96)

LEMONY ASPARAGUS AND PASTA SALAD

8 ounces penne pasta

1 pound asparagus, trimmed and cut diagonally into 2-inch pieces

2 tablespoons reduced-calorie mayonnaise

2 tablespoons defatted chicken broth or vegetable broth

1 tablespoon fresh lemon juice

2 teaspoons Dijon mustard

1 garlic clove, crushed

¼ teaspoon freshly ground black pepper

2 ounces shredded sharp Cheddar cheese

¼ cup diagonally sliced scallions

Finding pasta shapes that echo other ingredients in a recipe is part of the fun of creative pasta cookery. Asparagus spears, cut into 2-inch lengths, are much the same shape as penne, or pasta "quills." Similarly, carrot slices would work well with rotelli, or wagon-wheel pasta, and ribbons of zucchini or yellow squash with fettuccine. Here, the asparagus and pasta are cooked together: Be sure to add the asparagus before the penne is done so that the pasta does not overcook.

1 Bring a large covered pot of water to a boil over high heat. Add the pasta, return to a boil and cook for 10 to 12 minutes or according to package directions until al dente. About three minutes before the pasta is done, add the asparagus and cook until crisp-tender. Drain the pasta and asparagus in a colander, cool under cold running water and drain again.

2 In a salad bowl, whisk together the mayonnaise, broth, lemon juice, mustard, garlic and pepper. Add the pasta and asparagus, and toss to coat well. Sprinkle with the Cheddar and scallions, and serve.

Preparation time 10 minutes • **Total time** 25 minutes • **Per serving** 309 calories, 7.9 g. fat (23% of calories), 3.6 g. saturated fat, 17 mg. cholesterol, 241 mg. sodium, 2.1 g. dietary fiber, 133 mg. calcium, 3 mg. iron, 23 mg. vitamin C, 0.4 mg. beta-carotene • **Serves 4**

Cut the asparagus into pieces about the same size and shape as the penne.

SUBSTITUTION

Frozen asparagus can be used when fresh is not available. It's not necessary to cook the asparagus along with the pasta; just thaw it in the refrigerator, then place it in a colander and pour the boiling cooking liquid over it when you drain the pasta.

MARKET AND PANTRY

Asparagus can be expensive, so you want to be sure to get the best spears with the least waste. Look for plump stalks that are fresh and green all the way down: If the bottom of the stalk is hard, dry and white, it will be unusable. The tips of the spears should consist of tightly closed, moist-looking buds. The best way to store this delicate vegetable is to treat it as if it were a bouquet of flowers: Trim the bottoms of the stalks, then stand them in a tall container and add 1 inch of cold water. Cover with a plastic bag to hold in the moisture. Fresh asparagus will keep for about 3 days in the refrigerator.

Pasta with Cauliflower and Cheddar

8 ounces whole-wheat linguine

3 cups small cauliflower florets

1½ cups 1% low-fat milk

2 tablespoons cornstarch

½ teaspoon dry mustard

½ teaspoon freshly ground black pepper

¼ teaspoon dried thyme, crumbled

¼ teaspoon hot pepper sauce

⅛ teaspoon salt

4 ounces extra-sharp Cheddar cheese, shredded

2 tablespoons grated Parmesan cheese

¼ cup thinly sliced scallion greens

Ivory white cauliflower could almost pass for pasta, especially when blanketed with a creamy sauce, and it makes a most interesting meal when paired with sturdy whole-wheat linguine. Some "secret ingredients" help cut the fat content of the two-cheese sauce: It's based on a blend of low-fat milk and cornstarch (rather than whole milk), and the sharp Cheddar flavor is underscored with dry mustard and hot pepper sauce so that you use less cheese than usual.

1 Bring a large covered pot of water to a boil over high heat. Add the pasta, return to a boil and cook for 9 to 11 minutes, or according to package directions. Four minutes before the pasta is done, stir in the cauliflower and cook until the cauliflower is tender and the pasta is al dente. Reserving ½ cup of the cooking liquid, drain the pasta and cauliflower in a colander.

2 While the pasta is cooking, in a heavy medium saucepan, whisk together the milk, cornstarch, mustard, pepper, thyme, hot pepper sauce and salt until smooth. Place the pan over medium-high heat and bring to a boil, stirring constantly. Cook, stirring, for 1 minute, or until the sauce is quite thick; remove the pan from the heat.

3 Transfer the pasta and cauliflower to a warmed serving bowl; add the reserved pasta cooking liquid and toss to mix well.

4 Add the Cheddar and Parmesan to the sauce and whisk until smooth. Pour the sauce over the pasta and cauliflower, and toss to mix. Sprinkle with the scallions.

Preparation time 10 minutes • **Total time** 30 minutes • **Per serving** 401 calories, 12 g. fat (27% of calories), 7.3 g. saturated fat, 36 mg. cholesterol, 373 mg. sodium, 8.7 g. dietary fiber, 412 mg. calcium, 3 mg. iron, 56 mg. vitamin C, 0.3 mg. beta-carotene • **Serves 4**

KITCHEN TIPS

You'll need a head of cauliflower that weighs about 2 pounds to yield the 3 cups of florets required for this recipe. Take off any leaves and wash the head of cauliflower. Halve it, using a large, heavy knife, then remove the dense core. Break the head into large florets or cut them apart with a small knife. Then, if necessary, divide the florets into smaller sections.

PENNE WITH BROCCOLI AND CHICK-PEAS

1 tablespoon extra-virgin olive oil

2 large red onions, sliced

3 garlic cloves, minced

4 cups small broccoli florets

1 cup defatted reduced-sodium
chicken broth or vegetable
broth

8 ounces penne pasta

1 can (10½ ounces) chick-peas,
rinsed and drained or 1¼ cups
drained cooked chick-peas (see
below)

½ teaspoon freshly ground black
pepper

3 tablespoons freshly grated
Parmesan cheese

If using dried chick-peas (see directions at right), drain the soaking water and then add fresh water for cooking. This helps make the chick-peas easier to digest.

Chick-peas are a favorite legume around the Mediterranean. They are the main ingredient in the Middle Eastern fritters called *falafel* as well as *hummus*, a rich, creamy paste used as a sandwich spread or dip. The French prepare many soups, stews and salads with these nutty-tasting legumes, and a savory oversized pancake called *socca*, beloved in Nice, is made from chick-pea flour.

1 Bring a large covered pot of water to a boil over high heat.

2 Meanwhile, heat the oil in a large, deep skillet over high heat. Add the onions and garlic, and stir well to coat with the oil. Reduce the heat to medium and cook, stirring frequently, for 7 to 8 minutes, or until the onions are very tender and light golden brown. (Add a tablespoon of the broth if the pan gets too dry.)

3 Stir in the broccoli and broth; increase the heat to high and bring to a boil. Reduce the heat to medium-high, cover and simmer, stirring occasionally, for 6 to 7 minutes, or until the broccoli is tender.

4 Meanwhile, add the pasta to the boiling water, return to a boil and cook for 10 to 12 minutes or according to package directions until al dente. Reserving ¼ cup of the cooking liquid, drain the pasta in a colander.

5 Add the chick-peas and pepper to the broccoli and cook for 2 to 3 minutes, or until heated through. Add the penne and the reserved cooking liquid to the vegetables, and toss to coat the pasta. Transfer the mixture to a heated serving bowl and sprinkle with the Parmesan.

Preparation time 10 minutes • **Total time** 35 minutes • **Per serving** 404 calories, 7.7 g. fat (17% of calories), 1.6 g. saturated fat, 4 mg. cholesterol, 366 mg. sodium, 9.7 g. dietary fiber, 172 mg. calcium, 4 mg. iron, 102 mg. vitamin C, 1.3 mg. beta-carotene • **Serves 4**

KITCHEN TIP
Here's how to presoak and cook dried chick-peas: Place them in a large saucepan and add cold water to cover. Bring to a boil and cook for 2 minutes; cover and let stand for 1 hour. Drain, add fresh water (2 cups for each ½ cup of chick-peas) and bring to a boil. Simmer, partially covered, for about 90 minutes, or until the chick-peas are tender but firm.

FETTUCCINE WITH TOMATO-BASIL SAUCE

1 tablespoon extra-virgin olive oil

1 large onion, chopped

3-4 garlic cloves, minced

¼ teaspoon salt

¼ teaspoon freshly ground black pepper

¼ teaspoon crushed red pepper flakes (optional)

2 pounds ripe tomatoes, coarsely chopped in a food processor or by hand

3 tablespoons no-salt-added tomato paste

8 ounces spinach fettuccine

¾ cup coarsely chopped fresh basil, plus basil sprigs for garnish

2 tablespoons coarsely grated Parmesan cheese

Tomatoes and basil, which share the same season, make one of the most delicious combinations imaginable. To preserve their summer-fresh flavors in this dish, the tomatoes are cooked only briefly, and the basil is added at the last possible moment. The Parmesan that tops the pasta should be grated just before serving. Instead of using a grater, you can shave slivers of Parmesan with a swivel-bladed vegetable peeler, a cheese plane or a sharp paring knife.

1 Bring a large covered pot of water to a boil over high heat.

2 Meanwhile, warm the oil in a large, heavy saucepan over high heat. Add the onions and garlic, and sauté for 3 to 4 minutes, or until tender. Add the salt, black pepper and red pepper flakes (if using). Stir in the tomatoes and tomato paste, and bring to a boil. Reduce the heat to low, cover and simmer, stirring occasionally, for 15 minutes, or until the tomatoes begin to cook down into a sauce.

3 While the sauce simmers, add the pasta to the boiling water, return to a boil and cook for 9 to 11 minutes or according to package directions until al dente. Reserving ¼ cup of the cooking liquid, drain the pasta in a colander. Transfer the pasta to a warmed serving bowl and toss with the reserved cooking liquid.

4 Stir the chopped basil into the sauce and spoon the sauce over the pasta. Top with the Parmesan and garnish with the basil sprigs.

Preparation time 20 minutes • **Total time** 45 minutes • **Per serving** 353 calories, 8.1 g. fat (21% of calories), 1.8 g. saturated fat, 56 mg. cholesterol, 265 mg. sodium, 8.3 g. dietary fiber, 179 mg. calcium, 5 mg. iron, 55 mg. vitamin C, 1.4 mg. beta-carotene • **Serves 4**

There are several different varieties of basil. This "basil bouquet" is composed of common basil, also called sweet basil, and cinnamon basil, which has a uniquely spicy scent and flavor.

ON THE MENU
Although the spinach in the fettuccine contributes a vivid green color, it doesn't really "count" as a vegetable. So serve the pasta with steamed broccoli dressed with lemon juice and garlic; or chilled cooked zucchini and carrots tossed with a red-wine vinaigrette; or a big mixed salad.

MARKET AND PANTRY
The time to make this dish is when red-ripe tomatoes are at markets and farmstands. When you buy beautiful tomatoes, handle them with care. Store them at room temperature for no more than 2 to 3 days and never refrigerate them: The cold will destroy their flavor and texture.

BAKED PASTA PRIMAVERA

6 ounces ziti

2 cups small broccoli florets

1¼ cups diagonally sliced carrots

8 ounces asparagus, cut diagonally into 1-inch pieces

1 small zucchini, halved lengthwise and sliced ¼ inch thick

3 cans (8 ounces each) no-salt-added tomato sauce

¾ teaspoon dried Italian herb seasoning (see page 13)

¼ teaspoon freshly ground black pepper

¾ cup part-skim ricotta cheese

3 ounces shredded part-skim mozzarella cheese

2 tablespoons grated Parmesan cheese

The original recipe for pasta primavera was prepared with a light cream sauce, but this popular dish of pasta and vegetables is open to many variations. The basic idea is to use spring vegetables—such as asparagus or peas—or at least young, tender specimens of summer vegetables, such as the small broccoli florets and zucchini called for here.

1 Preheat the oven to 425°. Bring a large covered pot of water to a boil over high heat.

2 Add the ziti to the boiling water, return to a boil and cook for 9 minutes or according to package directions until al dente. Four minutes before the ziti is done, stir in the broccoli florets and carrots. Two minutes before the ziti is done, stir in the asparagus and zucchini. Cook until the pasta is al dente and the vegetables are crisp-tender. Drain in a colander.

3 In the pasta cooking pot, combine the tomato sauce, Italian seasoning and pepper; bring to a boil over high heat. Remove from the heat, stir in the pasta and vegetables, and toss until mixed. Pour the mixture into a 9 x 13-inch baking dish.

4 Spoon dollops of ricotta onto the pasta mixture, then sprinkle on the mozzarella and Parmesan. Bake for 12 to 15 minutes, or until the mozzarella is melted and the sauce is bubbly.

Preparation time 16 minutes • **Total time** 45 minutes • **Per serving** 393 calories, 9.5 g. fat (22% of calories), 5 g. saturated fat, 29 mg. cholesterol, 275 mg. sodium, 7.4 g. dietary fiber, 354 mg. calcium, 4 mg. iron, 89 mg. vitamin C, 8.2 mg. beta-carotene
Serves 4

KITCHEN TIPS
This recipe will save you time because it calls for adding the raw vegetables to the already-cooking pasta. However, adding cold ingredients could stop the boiling, so be sure to have the vegetables at room temperature.

HEADSTART
You can cut up the vegetables in advance and refrigerate them in plastic bags until needed. Combine the carrots and broccoli in one bag, the asparagus and zucchini in another. If time is really tight, buy cut-up vegetables at a salad bar.

Macaroni and Cheese Salad

6 ounces elbow macaroni

⅓ cup chopped fresh cilantro

¼ cup hot or medium salsa

3 tablespoons reduced-fat sour cream

Grated zest of 1 lime

2 tablespoons fresh lime juice

1 teaspoon ground cumin

½ teaspoon freshly ground black pepper

1 medium green bell pepper, diced

1 medium yellow or red bell pepper, diced

2 ounces shredded sharp Cheddar cheese

½ cup sliced scallions

Instead of a mayonnaise-dressed pasta salad, enliven your next buffet or barbecue with this colorful macaroni-and-vegetable mixture. Like the best party dishes, it can be made a day in advance, and the flavor will intensify if you prepare the salad ahead of time and refrigerate it overnight.

1 Bring a large covered pot of water to a boil over high heat. Add the pasta to the boiling water, return to a boil and cook for 7 to 9 minutes or according to package directions until al dente. Drain in a colander and rinse under cold running water; drain again.

2 While the pasta is cooking, in a salad bowl, whisk together the cilantro, salsa, sour cream, lime zest and juice, cumin and black pepper.

3 Add the macaroni, bell peppers, Cheddar and scallions to the dressing, and toss to combine.

Preparation time 12 minutes • **Total time** 25 minutes • **Per serving** 257 calories, 7 g. fat (25% of calories), 3.8 g. saturated fat, 19 mg. cholesterol, 185 mg. sodium, 2 g. dietary fiber, 131 mg. calcium, 3 mg. iron, 68 mg. vitamin C, 0.9 mg. beta-carotene
Serves 4

❧ ❧ ❧

This citrus zester shaves fine shreds of zest that are easy to measure in a spoon. Press the tool firmly against the fruit and pull it toward you.

This utensil, called a channel knife, cuts a thicker strip of zest, which can be chopped into smaller pieces for recipes or left whole for garnishing.

WATERCRESS AND TOMATO SPAGHETTI

1 cup water

1 ounce (½ cup) sun-dried tomatoes (not packed in oil)

2 teaspoons extra-virgin olive oil

6 scallions, thinly sliced

3 garlic cloves, minced

3 large ripe tomatoes (1½ pounds), coarsely chopped in a food processor or by hand

¼ teaspoon salt

⅛–¼ teaspoon crushed red pepper flakes

6 kalamata or ripe olives, sliced off pits

8 ounces spaghetti

1 bunch watercress, washed, tough stems removed

1 tablespoon grated Parmesan cheese

When tomatoes are dried—either in the sun or in special ovens—their flavor is concentrated, just as drying turns grapes into sugar-sweet raisins. The dried tomatoes, if not packed in oil, are usually softened by soaking them in boiling water before cooking. On their own, sun-dried tomatoes are a potent seasoning; in this recipe, they reinforce the flavor of fresh tomatoes.

1 Place the water and dried tomatoes in a small saucepan and bring to a boil over high heat. Remove from the heat and let stand for 5 minutes, or until softened. Drain the tomatoes, cool briefly under cold running water and cut into small pieces.

2 Bring a large covered pot of water to a boil over high heat.

3 Meanwhile, heat the oil in a large no-stick skillet over high heat. Add the scallions and garlic, and sauté for 1 to 2 minutes, or until the scallions have wilted. Stir in the fresh and dried tomatoes, the salt and red pepper, and cook until the tomatoes start to release their juices and the juices come to a boil. Reduce the heat to medium; cover and simmer, stirring occasionally, for 10 minutes, or until the flavors are blended. Stir in the olives.

4 While the sauce simmers, add the pasta to the boiling water, return to a boil and cook for 8 to 10 minutes or according to package directions until al dente. Drain in a colander.

5 Place the watercress in a warmed serving bowl. Add the pasta, then pour the sauce over the pasta. Toss to mix the ingredients and to wilt the watercress. Sprinkle the pasta with the Parmesan.

Preparation time 20 minutes • **Total time** 45 minutes • **Per serving** 318 calories, 5.2 g. fat (15% of calories), 1 g. saturated fat, 1.2 mg. cholesterol, 264 mg. sodium, 6.8 g. dietary fiber, 125 mg. calcium, 4 mg. iron, 77 mg. vitamin C, 2.7 mg. beta-carotene • **Serves 4**

FOR A CHANGE
Instead of watercress, toss the pasta with trimmed arugula, a long-leaved green with a similar mildly bitter flavor.

ON THE MENU
For a refreshing Italian-style dessert, finish the meal with lemon sorbet dusted with finely ground espresso powder.

GREEK-STYLE PASTA AND TOMATO SALAD

8 ounces corkscrew pasta

2½ ounces crumbled feta cheese

⅓ cup plain nonfat yogurt

1 tablespoon fresh lemon juice

¾ teaspoon dried mint

¼ teaspoon ground cumin

¼ teaspoon freshly ground black pepper

⅛ teaspoon salt

1 garlic clove, peeled

1 bunch watercress, washed, tough stems removed

2 cups halved cherry tomatoes

½ cup sliced radishes

Most people have sampled Greek salad, a flavorful toss of greens, cucumbers, tomatoes, ripe olives and tangy feta cheese with a dressing made of Greek olive oil, lemon juice and oregano. For this hearty pasta salad, feta cheese is used in a creamy yogurt-based dressing that is served over pasta, watercress, tomatoes and radishes.

1 Bring a large covered pot of water to a boil over high heat. Add the pasta to the boiling water, return to a boil and cook for 11 to 13 minutes or according to package directions until al dente. Drain in a colander and rinse under cold running water; drain again. Transfer to a salad bowl.

2 While the pasta cooks, combine the feta, yogurt, lemon juice, mint, cumin, pepper and salt in a food processor or blender. With the machine running, drop the garlic clove through the feed tube and process until the dressing is smooth.

3 Pour the dressing over the pasta. Add the watercress, cherry tomatoes and radishes, and toss to coat well.

Preparation time 15 minutes • **Total time** 30 minutes • **Per serving** 288 calories, 5 g. fat (16% of calories), 2.8 g. saturated fat, 16 mg. cholesterol, 311 mg. sodium, 3.3 g. dietary fiber, 195 mg. calcium, 3 mg. iron, 33 mg. vitamin C, 1.4 mg. beta-carotene
Serves 4

❧ ❧ ❧

Cut the thick stems from the watercress at the point where the bunch is tied.

Holding the cress by the remaining stems, rinse the leaves in a basin of water.

RAVIOLI WITH PEAS AND RED PEPPERS

½ cup defatted reduced-sodium chicken broth

1 package (10 ounces) frozen peas

¼ cup loosely packed Italian parsley sprigs

1 garlic clove, peeled

¼ teaspoon freshly ground black pepper

9 ounces fresh or frozen cheese ravioli

1 medium red bell pepper, diced

2 teaspoons grated Parmesan cheese

You don't need to make your own pasta in order to serve it fresh: Small pasta shops are springing up everywhere, offering such specialties as pumpkin ravioli, wild-mushroom tortellini and broccoli-rabe agnolotti. Cooking times vary for filled pastas; you need to know the approximate time in advance so you can cook the bell peppers and peas in the same pot as the ravioli without overcooking either the vegetables or the pasta. If directions don't come with fresh ravioli, be sure to ask about the recommended cooking time.

1 Bring a large covered pot of water to a boil over high heat.

2 Meanwhile, in a small saucepan, combine the broth, 1 cup of the peas, the parsley sprigs and garlic. Cover and bring to a boil over high heat. Cook for 1 minute; remove from the heat.

3 Purée the pea mixture in a food processor or blender until very smooth; stir in the black pepper and set aside.

4 Add the ravioli to the boiling water and return to a boil, stirring frequently. Cook for 4 to 5 minutes, or according to package directions. Two minutes before the ravioli are done, add the bell peppers and the remaining 1 cup peas to the pot. Return to a boil and cook for 2 minutes longer, or until the peppers are crisp-tender, the peas are heated through, and the ravioli are tender. Drain in a colander and transfer to a warmed serving bowl.

5 Add the pea purée to the ravioli and toss gently to combine. Sprinkle with the Parmesan.

Preparation time 12 minutes • **Total time** 30 minutes • **Per serving** 272 calories, 9 g. fat (30% of calories), 4.7 g. saturated fat, 57 mg. cholesterol, 450 mg. sodium, 3.2 g. dietary fiber, 188 mg. calcium, 3 mg. iron, 52 mg. vitamin C, 1.1 mg. beta-carotene
Serves 4

KITCHEN TIPS
It's not necessary to thaw frozen peas, and they will probably turn mushy if you do. The peas take only minutes to cook, and if you're using them in a salad, you don't even need to cook them—just place them in a strainer and rinse them under cold tap water. Frozen peas straight from the freezer are a great snack—one even vegetable-spurning kids may like.

PIZZA PASTA

2 large green bell peppers, cut into quarters

8 ounces spaghetti

4 ounces fresh mushrooms, sliced

3 tablespoons defatted chicken broth

3 cans (8 ounces each) no-salt-added tomato sauce

1 teaspoon dried Italian herb seasoning (see page 13)

¼ teaspoon garlic powder

⅛ teaspoon salt

⅛ teaspoon crushed red pepper flakes

4 ounces shredded part-skim mozzarella cheese

2 tablespoons grated Parmesan cheese

The flavors of pizza are instantly identifiable, but it's a treat to taste them in a new context. Here, spaghetti is baked with classic pizza ingredients: tomato sauce, garlic, mozzarella, peppers, mushrooms and Parmesan. Use a store-bought Italian herb seasoning, or make your own, using the recipe on page 13.

1 Bring a large covered pot of water to a boil over high heat. Preheat the broiler and a broiler pan and rack.

2 Arrange the peppers in a single layer on the broiler-pan rack and broil 2 to 3 inches from the heat, turning once, for 8 to 10 minutes, or until the peppers are tender and very lightly charred. Transfer the peppers to a cutting board and set aside to cool slightly, then cut each quarter into 4 pieces.

3 While the peppers are broiling, add the pasta to the boiling water, return to a boil and cook for 9 to 11 minutes or according to package directions until al dente. Drain the pasta in a colander.

4 In the pasta cooking pot, combine the mushrooms and broth, and bring to a boil over high heat. Sauté for 4 to 6 minutes, or until the mushrooms are tender.

5 Stir in the tomato sauce, roasted peppers, Italian seasoning, garlic powder, salt and crushed red pepper. Reduce the heat to medium-high and bring to a simmer, then reduce the heat to medium-low, cover and simmer for 5 minutes to blend the flavors.

6 Add the spaghetti to the sauce and toss to coat well. Transfer the mixture to a 9 x 13-inch flameproof baking pan or a 2-quart flameproof oval baking dish; sprinkle with the mozzarella and Parmesan, and broil, watching closely, for 1 to 3 minutes, or until the cheeses are melted and the sauce is bubbly.

Preparation time 10 minutes • **Total time** 40 minutes • **Per serving** 378 calories, 7.2 g. fat (17% of calories), 3.5 g. saturated fat, 18 mg. cholesterol, 341 mg. sodium, 5 g. dietary fiber, 235 mg. calcium, 4 mg. iron, 73 mg. vitamin C, 1.5 mg. beta-carotene • **Serves 4**

SHELLS WITH DOUBLE-MUSHROOM SAUCE

½ ounce (¼ cup) dried mushrooms

1 cup boiling water

1 tablespoon olive oil

¾ cup diced shallots or chopped scallions (white parts only)

3 garlic cloves, minced

½ teaspoon freshly ground black pepper

½ teaspoon dried thyme

12 ounces white button mushrooms, coarsely chopped in a food processor or by hand

1 cup defatted reduced-sodium chicken broth

1 tablespoon plus 2 teaspoons cornstarch dissolved in 2 tablespoons dry white wine or water

6 ounces medium pasta shells or penne pasta

¼ cup chopped fresh Italian parsley

2 tablespoons grated Parmesan cheese

Even the cheapest dried mushrooms, sold in supermarkets, have a deeply savory, woodsy taste. Cook them with white button mushrooms and you might think you're eating fresh wild mushrooms, which are indeed a luxury item. If the dried mushrooms are in large pieces, chop them after soaking; if small, use them as is.

1 Put the dried mushrooms in a large glass measuring cup. Pour the boiling water over them and let stand for 5 minutes, or until softened. Meanwhile, line a small strainer with cheesecloth.

2 Using a slotted spoon, lift the mushrooms out of the soaking liquid and transfer them to small bowl. Place the strainer over the bowl and pour the soaking liquid through it, leaving the sediment in the cup.

3 Bring a large covered pot of water to a boil over high heat.

4 Meanwhile, in a large, heavy saucepan, warm the oil over medium-high heat. Add the shallots or scallions and garlic, and sauté for 3 to 4 minutes, or until the shallots are tender. Stir in the pepper and thyme, then the fresh mushrooms, and sauté for 5 minutes, or until the mushrooms release their juices.

5 Add the dried mushrooms and mushroom soaking liquid, the broth and the cornstarch mixture to the pan, and bring to a boil; cook, stirring constantly, for 1 to 3 minutes, or until thickened. Reduce heat to low, cover and simmer, stirring occasionally, for 15 minutes, or until the flavors are blended.

6 Meanwhile, add the pasta to the boiling water, return to a boil and cook for 8 to 10 minutes or according to package directions until al dente. Drain the pasta in a colander and transfer to a warmed serving bowl. Pour the sauce over the pasta, sprinkle with the parsley and Parmesan, and serve.

Preparation time 11 minutes • **Total time** 45 minutes • **Per serving** 278 calories, 5.7 g. fat (19% of calories), 1.2 g. saturated fat, 2.4 mg. cholesterol, 231 mg. sodium, 2.6 g. dietary fiber, 82 mg. calcium, 4 mg. iron, 10 mg. vitamin C, 0.1 mg. beta-carotene • **Serves 4**

❧ ❧ ❧

PASTA SALAD WITH CHICK-PEAS

1 pound ripe tomatoes

1 medium cucumber, peeled and diced

¼ cup chopped red onions

2 tablespoons chopped fresh dill

2 tablespoons chopped fresh mint

1 tablespoon extra-virgin olive oil

1 tablespoon red wine vinegar

1 small garlic clove, crushed

½ teaspoon freshly ground black pepper

¼ teaspoon salt

1 can (19 ounces) chick-peas, rinsed and drained

8 ounces fresh spinach linguine, cut in half

You'll find fresh pasta in many supermarkets, in the dairy section or in a special display with ready-made sauces. If you don't use fresh pasta right away, wrap it airtight and store it in the refrigerator for up to one week or in the freezer for up to a month.

1 Bring a medium saucepan of water to a boil over high heat. One at a time, add the tomatoes and blanch for 20 seconds, or until the skins begin to wrinkle. Cool the tomatoes in a bowl of cold water and slip off the skins. Coarsely chop the tomatoes and place in a salad bowl.

2 Add the cucumber, onions, dill, mint, oil, vinegar, garlic, pepper and salt to the tomatoes, and mix well; stir in the chick-peas. Cover and let stand at room temperature for 10 minutes.

3 Return the water in the pot to a boil, add the pasta and bring to a boil again. Cook, stirring frequently, for 3 to 5 minutes, or until the pasta floats to the surface and is al dente. Drain in a colander and rinse briefly under cold running water.

4 Add the pasta to the chick-pea mixture and toss thoroughly.

Preparation time 15 minutes • **Total time** 35 minutes • **Per serving** 323 calories, 8.2 g. fat (23% of calories), 0.7 g. saturated fat, 64 mg. cholesterol, 345 mg. sodium, 5.4 g. dietary fiber, 87 mg. calcium, 4 mg. iron, 28 mg. vitamin C, 0.5 mg. beta-carotene • **Serves 4**

Drop a tomato into the pot of boiling water; remove it when the skin wrinkles.

After the tomato has cooled slightly, you can easily peel off the skin.

PASTA WITH ESCAROLE AND CANNELLINI

1 tablespoon extra-virgin olive oil

1 medium onion, chopped

1 large carrot, diced

2 large celery stalks with leaves, diced

3–4 garlic cloves, crushed

½–¾ teaspoon freshly ground black pepper

½ teaspoon dried basil, crumbled

¼ teaspoon salt

6 cups loosely packed cut escarole (1-inch pieces), well washed

½ cup defatted chicken or vegetable broth

1 can (19 ounces) cannellini beans, rinsed and drained

8 ounces pasta twists

Escarole's ruffled pale-green leaves have a slight bitterness reminiscent of the taste of chicory, a close relative. The inner leaves have a milder flavor than the outer leaves. Although escarole is often used in salads, it is delicious when braised in broth and served as a side dish or, as it is here, partnered with pasta and white beans.

1 Bring a large covered pot of water to a boil over high heat.

2 Meanwhile, warm the oil in a large, heavy saucepan over medium-high heat. Stir in the onions, carrots, celery and garlic, and sauté for 1 minute. Add the pepper, basil and salt, and reduce the heat to medium-low; cover and cook, stirring frequently, for 5 to 7 minutes, or until the vegetables are tender.

3 Add the escarole and broth to the vegetables, and raise the heat to high. Cook, tossing frequently, for 2 to 3 minutes, or until the escarole is wilted. Stir in the beans and reduce the heat to medium; cover and simmer for 3 to 5 minutes, or until the beans are heated through.

4 Meanwhile, add the pasta to the boiling water, return to a boil and cook for 10 to 12 minutes or according to package directions until al dente. Reserving 2 tablespoons of the cooking liquid, drain the pasta in a colander.

5 Combine the pasta, the reserved cooking liquid and the escarole mixture in a heated serving bowl, and toss to combine well.

Preparation time 15 minutes • **Total time** 35 minutes • **Per serving** 390 calories, 5.6 g. fat (13% of calories), 0.7 g. saturated fat, 0 mg. cholesterol, 483 mg. sodium, 11 g. dietary fiber, 126 mg. calcium, 5 mg. iron, 15 mg. vitamin C, 5.4 mg. beta-carotene • **Serves 4**

FOR A CHANGE

Fennel, which is very similar to celery in texture, has a mild licorice-like flavor that would add a new dimension to this dish. Use 1 cup of diced fennel to replace the celery.

NUTRITION NOTE

When choosing greens, the general rule is: The darker the leaves, the more nutritious. Escarole, for instance, is a richer source of beta-carotene, vitamin C and calcium than iceberg lettuce.

NOODLES WITH KALE AND POTATOES

2 teaspoons olive oil

1 teaspoon unsalted butter or margarine

6 packed cups torn kale, tough stems removed

1 large onion, sliced

8 ounces small new potatoes, cut into wedges

1 cup defatted reduced-sodium chicken broth or vegetable broth

1 teaspoon caraway seeds

½ teaspoon freshly ground black pepper

¼ teaspoon salt

6 ounces wide egg noodles

2 scallions, thinly sliced

I n the days when "starches" were considered fattening, a dish made with both noodles and potatoes would have been out of the question. Now, however, we recognize starches as energy-giving complex carbohydrates and know that they should make up the greatest proportion of our daily diets.

1 Bring a large covered pot of water to a boil over high heat.

2 Meanwhile, heat the oil and butter in a large, heavy saucepan over medium-high heat until the butter melts. Stir in the kale and onions, and sauté for 2 to 3 minutes, or until the kale is wilted.

3 Stir in the potatoes, broth, caraway seeds, pepper and salt; increase the heat to high and bring to a boil. Reduce the heat to medium-low, cover and simmer, stirring occasionally, for 20 to 22 minutes, or until the potatoes are tender.

4 When the potatoes are nearly done, add the noodles to the boiling water and return to a boil. Cook for 4 to 6 minutes or according to package directions until al dente. Drain in a colander and transfer to a warmed serving bowl.

5 Spoon the vegetable mixture over the noodles and sprinkle with the scallions.

Preparation time 12 minutes • **Total time** 45 minutes • **Per serving** 332 calories, 6.4 g. fat (17% of calories), 1.4 g. saturated fat, 43 mg. cholesterol, 366 mg. sodium, 11.6 g. dietary fiber, 208 mg. calcium, 5 mg. iron, 167 mg. vitamin C, 6.9 mg. beta-carotene • **Serves 4**

To stem kale, fold the leaves forward and hold them near the stem; pull the stem from bottom to top so it peels off the top portion of the midrib along with the stem. Young kale does not require stemming if the leaves and stems are tender.

FOOD FACT
New potatoes are any variety of potatoes—red or white, baking or boiling—that have been recently dug and not stored. They have a thin "feathering" skin.

SUBSTITUTION
If kale is not available, use green cabbage, cut into narrow strips.

NUTRITION NOTE
Kale, a nutritional superstar, is an excellent source of vitamin C, calcium, beta-carotene and iron.

MARKET AND PANTRY
Look for deep green kale with no yellowed or withered leaves. Wrap the kale in damp paper towels, then in a plastic bag.

Pasta with Seafood

❧ ❧ ❧

A TEMPTING VARIETY, FROM

A COMFORTING SALMON-NOODLE

CASSEROLE TO AN ELEGANT

SCALLOP SAUTÉ

ANGEL HAIR WITH GRILLED SALMON

- 1½ teaspoons ground cumin
- ¼ teaspoon freshly ground black pepper
- ⅛ teaspoon salt
- 8 ounces salmon fillet, halved lengthwise, then cut crosswise into ½-inch-thick pieces
- 2 garlic cloves, minced
- 1½ teaspoons extra-virgin olive oil
- 1 small bay leaf, preferably Turkish
- ⅛ teaspoon fennel seeds
- 1 can (16 ounces) crushed tomatoes in purée
- 2 tablespoons frozen orange juice concentrate
- 2 teaspoons fresh lemon juice
- 8 ounces angel-hair (capelli d'angelo) pasta
- 1 package (10 ounces) frozen French-cut green beans, thawed

Salmon fillets may have tiny "feather bones" remaining in the flesh; these should be removed. Find them by running your fingers along the center portion of the top surface of the fish.

1 Bring a large covered pot of water to a boil over high heat. Preheat the broiler and spray a jelly-roll pan with no-stick spray.

2 In a cup, mix ¾ teaspoon of the cumin, ⅛ teaspoon of the pepper and the salt. Sprinkle the spice mixture over both sides of the salmon; arrange the salmon in a single layer in the prepared pan. Cover and let stand at room temperature for about 10 minutes.

3 Meanwhile, in a heavy, medium saucepan, combine the garlic, 1 teaspoon of the oil, the bay leaf, fennel seeds and the remaining ¾ teaspoon cumin and ⅛ teaspoon pepper. Cook, stirring, over high heat for 1 to 2 minutes, or until the garlic is fragrant and the mixture sizzles.

4 Stir in the tomatoes and orange juice concentrate, and bring to a boil; reduce the heat to low, cover and simmer, stirring occasionally, for 10 minutes, or until the flavors are blended. Remove the pan from the heat; remove and discard the bay leaf.

5 Drizzle the salmon with the lemon juice and broil 3 to 4 inches from the heat for 2 to 3 minutes, without turning, until the fish flakes easily with a fork. Remove from the broiler.

6 Add the pasta to the boiling water, return to a boil and cook for 2 minutes; add the green beans and cook, stirring frequently, for 2 to 3 minutes longer, or until the pasta is al dente and the beans are heated through. Drain the pasta and beans in a colander; transfer to a heated serving bowl and toss with the remaining ½ teaspoon oil. Add the sauce to the pasta and beans, and toss to coat. Add the salmon and any juices that have collected in the pan and toss gently.

Preparation time 15 minutes • **Total time** 40 minutes • **Per serving** 380 calories, 6.6 g. fat (16% of calories), 1 g. saturated fat, 31 mg. cholesterol, 282 mg. sodium, 2.7 g. dietary fiber, 102 mg. calcium, 4 mg. iron, 41 mg. vitamin C, 0.7 mg. beta-carotene
Serves 4

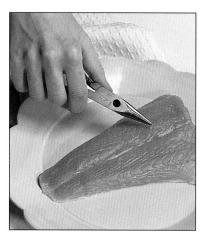

Use needle-nose pliers or tweezers to remove feather bones, which run from the center outward on the top of the fillet.

Preceding pages: Noodles with Shrimp and Bok Choy (recipe on page 116).

PASTA WITH SHRIMP AND BROCCOLI RABE

1 tablespoon olive oil

1 large onion, thinly sliced

3 garlic cloves, minced

6 ounces fusilli bucati or regular fusilli pasta

6 cups trimmed, cut-up broccoli rabe (2-inch lengths) or 4 cups broccoli florets

½ cup defatted chicken broth

12 ounces medium shrimp, peeled and deveined, tails left on

1 cup sliced roasted red peppers (from a jar)

½ teaspoon freshly ground black pepper

⅛ teaspoon salt

Fusilli—springy pasta "spindles"—come in several versions, long and short, solid and hollow, plain or colored with tomato or spinach; any of these would be fine for this dish. Hollow fusilli are called *fusilli bucati* or *fusilli col buco,* implying that their centers have been pierced or drilled out. If you'd like to use freshly roasted bell peppers for this recipe, follow the method given on page 49.

1 Bring a large covered pot of water to a boil over high heat.

2 Meanwhile, in a large, heavy saucepan, warm the oil over high heat. Add the onions and garlic, and toss to coat well with the oil. Reduce the heat to medium-low, cover and simmer, stirring occasionally, for 10 minutes, or until the onions are very tender.

3 Add the pasta to the boiling water, return to a boil and cook for 10 to 12 minutes or according to package directions until al dente. Drain the pasta in a colander and transfer to a warmed serving bowl.

4 While the pasta is cooking, add the broccoli rabe and broth to the onions; increase the heat to medium-high and bring to a boil. Cook, tossing frequently, for 3 to 4 minutes, or until the broccoli rabe is tender.

5 Add the shrimp, roasted peppers, black pepper and salt to the broccoli rabe and cook, tossing frequently, for 3 to 4 minutes, or until the shrimp are pink and just cooked through.

6 Pour the sauce over the pasta, toss to coat well and serve.

Broccoli rabe, also called *rapini,* is wonderful with pasta. It is usually blanched or sautéed to tone down its assertive, slightly bitter flavor.

Preparation time 22 minutes • **Total time** 40 minutes • **Per serving** 328 calories, 6 g. fat (16% of calories), 0.8 g. saturated fat, 105 mg. cholesterol, 357 mg. sodium, 4.9 g. dietary fiber, 138 mg. calcium, 6 mg. iron, 118 mg. vitamin C, 3.1 mg. beta-carotene • **Serves 4**

ZITI WITH HERBED SWORDFISH

8 ounces swordfish, cut into
1-inch cubes

3 garlic cloves, crushed

1 teaspoon grated lemon zest

¾ teaspoon dried rosemary,
crumbled

¼ teaspoon freshly ground black
pepper

Large pinch of crushed red
pepper flakes (optional)

2 teaspoons extra-virgin olive oil

1 medium onion, chopped

1 can (14½ ounces) no-salt-added
stewed tomatoes

1 medium yellow summer squash,
halved lengthwise and cut into
¼-inch slices

½ cup defatted chicken broth

2 tablespoons fresh lemon juice

6 ounces ziti pasta

People who adore beef usually love swordfish, too, for this big saltwater fish, caught on both coasts, has dark, "meaty" flesh. Because swordfish is dense and firm, it can be cut into chunks that hold their shape whether they're simmered, stir-fried or skewered.

1 Bring a large covered pot of water to a boil over high heat.

2 Place the swordfish on a large plate and mix with 1 crushed garlic clove, the lemon zest, ¼ teaspoon of the rosemary, ⅛ teaspoon of the black pepper and the pepper flakes (if using). Cover and let stand at room temperature for 10 minutes.

3 Meanwhile, in a large, heavy saucepan, warm the oil over high heat until hot but not smoking. Stir in the onions and the remaining 2 garlic cloves, and sauté for 4 to 5 minutes, or until the onions are tender.

4 Add the stewed tomatoes, summer squash, broth, lemon juice, the remaining ½ teaspoon rosemary and remaining ⅛ teaspoon pepper, and bring to a boil. Reduce the heat to medium, cover and simmer, stirring occasionally, for 5 minutes, or until the squash is tender and the flavors are blended.

5 Meanwhile, add the pasta to the boiling water, return to a boil and cook for 10 to 12 minutes or according to package directions until al dente. Reserving ½ cup of the cooking liquid, drain the pasta in a colander. Transfer the pasta to a large heated serving bowl and toss with the reserved cooking liquid.

6 Add the swordfish cubes to the sauce, cover and simmer gently for 3 to 4 minutes, or until the fish is opaque in the center. Spoon the sauce and fish over the pasta.

Preparation time 10 minutes • **Total time** 45 minutes • **Per serving** 307 calories, 5.8 g. fat (17% of calories), 1.1 g. saturated fat, 22 mg. cholesterol, 198 mg. sodium, 4.6 g. dietary fiber, 71 mg. calcium, 3 mg. iron, 26 mg. vitamin C, 0.5 mg. beta-carotene • **Serves 4**

Picnic Macaroni-Tuna Salad

6 ounces elbow macaroni

¼ cup plain nonfat yogurt

2 tablespoons reduced-calorie mayonnaise

2 tablespoons snipped fresh dill

2 tablespoons red wine vinegar

1 teaspoon Dijon mustard

½ teaspoon freshly ground black pepper

1 can (6⅛ ounces) water-packed tuna, drained

1 can (15 ounces) black beans, rinsed and drained

1 medium red bell pepper, diced

2 large celery stalks, sliced

¼ cup sliced radishes

¼ cup chopped red onion

Just about any mayonnaise-based salad dressing can be lightened by substituting low-fat or nonfat yogurt for all or some of the mayo. In this case, nonfat yogurt is combined with reduced-calorie mayonnaise; the addition of fresh dill, vinegar and mustard ensures that not a bit of flavor is lost even though the fat content is considerably reduced. Crunchy celery, bell peppers, radishes and red onion add up to an unusually appetizing macaroni salad, and black beans make this dish a nutritional superstar.

1 Bring a large covered pot of water to a boil over high heat. Add the pasta, return to a boil and cook for 8 to 9 minutes or according to package directions until al dente. Drain in a colander and cool briefly under gently running cold water; drain again.

2 In a salad bowl, whisk together the yogurt, mayonnaise, dill, vinegar, mustard and black pepper.

3 Break the tuna into flakes and put it in a small strainer. Rinse under cold running water and drain well.

4 Add the macaroni, tuna, beans, bell peppers, celery, radishes and onions to the salad bowl, and toss to coat with the dressing.

Preparation time 23 minutes • **Total time** 35 minutes • **Per serving** 314 calories, 3.6 g. fat (10% of calories), 0.7 g. saturated fat, 19 mg. cholesterol, 427 mg. sodium, 5 g. dietary fiber, 86 mg. calcium, 5 mg. iron, 41 mg. vitamin C, 0.7 mg. beta-carotene
Serves 4

Kitchen shears or regular scissors make quick work of mincing herbs such as dill. Pat the herbs thoroughly dry after rinsing them so that the leaves do not stick to the scissor blades.

ON THE MENU
Serve the salad on a bed of curly greens and accompany it with wedges of juicy ripe tomato.

NUTRITION NOTE
The majority of Americans don't need to worry about consuming too much protein; in fact, most get more protein than necessary, with an unfortunate bonus of saturated fat and cholesterol if red meat is the main source of protein. This macaroni salad is a fine example of a more healthful way to eat protein: One serving supplies 22 grams of protein, or about half the daily requirement for the average woman, but has less than 4 grams of fat. Most of the protein in the salad comes from the tuna, macaroni and beans. These ingredients also provide good amounts of iron, a mineral that many people think they can get only by eating red meat.

NOODLE BAKE WITH SALMON AND PEAS

1 tablespoon unsalted butter or margarine

2 large celery stalks, diced

6 scallions, thinly sliced

¼ cup plus 1 tablespoon all-purpose flour

½ teaspoon dried tarragon, crumbled

½ teaspoon freshly ground black pepper

1½ cups skim milk

½ cup defatted reduced-sodium chicken broth

6 ounces wide egg noodles

1 can (7½ ounces) red salmon

1 cup frozen peas

3 tablespoons diced roasted red pepper

1 tablespoon unseasoned dry bread crumbs

1 tablespoon grated Parmesan cheese

Anyone with fond memories of tuna-noodle casserole will delight in this flavorful lower-fat update. Be sure to undercook the noodles slightly so that they don't turn mushy when baked.

1 Preheat the oven to 425°. Spray a 2-quart casserole with no-stick spray. Bring a large covered pot of water to a boil over high heat.

2 In a heavy, medium saucepan, melt the butter or margarine over medium heat. Stir in the celery and scallions, and sauté for 3 minutes, or until the vegetables are tender. Sprinkle in the flour, tarragon and pepper, and cook, stirring constantly, for 1 minute. Pour in the milk and broth, and whisk to blend well. Remove the pan from the heat, cover and set aside for 1 minute. (This helps make the sauce smooth.)

3 Place the uncovered pan of sauce over high heat and bring to a boil, whisking frequently. Cook, stirring constantly, for 2 to 3 minutes, or until thickened. Remove from the heat, cover and keep warm.

4 Add the noodles to the boiling water and return to a boil. Cook for just 3 to 4 minutes. Reserving ¼ cup of the cooking liquid, drain the noodles in a colander. Cool briefly under cold running water, separating the noodles with your fingers.

5 While the noodles are cooking, rinse and drain the salmon. Remove any skin and large bones, then break the salmon into large flakes.

6 Pour the sauce into the noodle cooking pot. Add the noodles and the reserved ¼ cup cooking liquid, and toss gently. Add the salmon, peas and roasted red peppers, and toss gently to mix. Transfer the mixture to the prepared casserole.

7 Mix together the bread crumbs and Parmesan, and sprinkle over the noodles. Bake for 15 to 20 minutes, or until the sauce is bubbly and the top is lightly browned.

Preparation time 5 minutes • **Total time** 45 minutes • **Per serving** 380 calories, 9.1 g. fat (21% of calories), 3.3 g. saturated fat, 70 mg. cholesterol, 473 mg. sodium, 3.9 g. dietary fiber, 291 mg. calcium, 4 mg. iron, 24 mg. vitamin C, 0.6 mg. beta-carotene • **Serves 4**

Noodles with Shrimp and Bok Choy

1 cup defatted reduced-sodium chicken broth

½ cup water

1 tablespoon dry sherry (optional)

2 garlic cloves, crushed

1 tablespoon grated fresh ginger

2 teaspoons reduced-sodium soy sauce

1 teaspoon dark sesame oil

1 medium fresh jalapeño pepper, cut in half

12 ounces small or medium shrimp (thawed if frozen), peeled and deveined

6 ounces fresh or dried capellini pasta

6 cups cut-up bok choy or napa cabbage (1-inch pieces)

½ cup drained canned sliced water chestnuts

¼ cup thinly sliced scallion greens

Capellini stands in for thin Chinese noodles in this pasta-in-broth meal. Fresh capellini is the quickest-cooking pasta of all: Test it after three minutes by biting a strand; if the pasta is properly al dente, drain and rinse it immediately to keep it from over-cooking. To freshen the flavor of the water chestnuts, drain them and place them in a small strainer, then pour some of the cooking liquid over them when you drain the pasta. Or simply drain the water chestnuts and rinse them under cool running water.

1 Bring a large covered pot of water to a boil over high heat.

2 In a large, heavy saucepan, combine the broth, water, sherry (if using), garlic, ginger, soy sauce, sesame oil and the jalapeño; cover and bring to a boil over high heat. Reduce the heat to medium-low and simmer for 5 minutes to blend the flavors. Remove and discard the jalapeño.

3 While the broth is simmering, remove the tails from the shrimp, if necessary. Cut the shrimp into 1-inch pieces.

4 Add the pasta to the boiling water, return to a boil and cook for 3 to 5 minutes or according to package directions until al dente. Drain in a colander and rinse briefly under cold running water; drain again.

5 Stir the shrimp, bok choy or napa cabbage and water chestnuts into the broth. Increase the heat to high and bring to a simmer, stirring frequently. Reduce the heat to low and cook, stirring frequently, for 3 to 5 minutes, or until the shrimp are pink and the bok choy is just crisp-tender.

6 Divide the pasta among 4 large, warmed soup bowls. Divide the broth, shrimp and vegetables among the 4 bowls and sprinkle each portion with scallions.

Preparation time 20 minutes • **Total time** 40 minutes • **Per serving** 240 calories, 3.8 g. fat (14% of calories), 0.6 g. saturated fat, 136 mg. cholesterol, 444 mg. sodium, 1 g. dietary fiber, 159 mg. calcium, 4 mg. iron, 55 mg. vitamin C, 2 mg. beta-carotene
Serves 4

MEDITERRANEAN SEASHELL SALAD

2 tablespoons frozen apple juice concentrate

2 tablespoons chopped fresh Italian parsley

1 tablespoon coarse Dijon mustard

1 tablespoon extra-virgin olive oil

1 tablespoon red wine vinegar

½ teaspoon ground cumin

¼ teaspoon freshly ground black pepper

1 medium yellow or red bell pepper, thinly sliced

1 cup thinly sliced fennel or celery

¼ cup thinly sliced red onions

6 ounces medium pasta shells

3 tablespoons golden raisins

1 can (3¾ ounces) water-pack sardines, drained and gently rinsed

Fresh sardines, quickly grilled, broiled or fried, are a great delicacy, and the tiny iridescent fish are a highlight of summer meals around the Mediterranean basin. In Sicily, filleted sardines are combined with macaroni, sweet fennel, onions, pine nuts and golden raisins—a typically Sicilian juxtaposition of sweet and savory flavors—in a casserole called *pasta con le sarde.* This unbaked version of the dish is made with canned sardines and a sprightly apple-juice dressing. A timesaving trick: The raisins are plumped by adding them to the pasta during the last few moments of cooking time.

1 Bring a large covered pot of water to a boil over high heat.

2 Meanwhile, in a salad bowl, whisk together the apple juice concentrate, parsley, mustard, oil, vinegar, cumin and black pepper.

3 Add the bell peppers, fennel or celery and onions to the dressing, and stir to blend. Cover and let stand at room temperature for 10 minutes.

4 While the vegetables marinate, add the pasta to the boiling water, return to a boil and cook for 9 to 11 minutes or according to package directions until al dente. One minute before the pasta is done, add the raisins. Drain the pasta and raisins in a colander, rinse briefly under cold running water and drain again.

5 Add the pasta and raisins to the salad bowl, and toss to mix. Add the sardines and toss gently.

Preparation time 10 minutes • **Total time** 25 minutes • **Per serving** 303 calories, 9.1 g. fat (27% of calories), 0.6 g. saturated fat, 0 mg. cholesterol, 178 mg. sodium, 2.2 g. dietary fiber, 111 mg. calcium, 3 mg. iron, 49 mg. vitamin C, 0.7 mg. beta-carotene • **Serves 4**

A fennel bulb, like a bunch of celery, is made up of many layers, so when you slice it crosswise it will fall into thin strips.

NUTRITION NOTE
Sardines have a lot to offer nutritionally. Although they are higher in fat than tuna, the fat is rich in omega-3s, polyunsaturated fatty acids that may be protective against heart disease. In addition, sardines are rich in iron, and the bone-in types are an excellent source of calcium.

Linguine with Scallops Provençale

8 ounces fresh linguine

⅓ cup defatted reduced-sodium chicken broth plus ⅓ cup water

1 tablespoon plus ½ teaspoon extra-virgin olive oil

1 large onion, thinly sliced

1 medium red bell pepper, thinly sliced

1 medium green bell pepper, thinly sliced

3 garlic cloves, minced

12 ounces sea scallops, tough muscle removed

2 cups halved cherry tomatoes

1 medium zucchini, cut into ¼-inch-thick slices

1 tablespoon fresh lemon juice

½ teaspoon freshly ground black pepper

¼ teaspoon salt

½ cup coarsely chopped fresh basil

From Provence, in southwestern France, come dishes that speak of the sun. Olives and olive oil are hallmarks of robustly flavored Provençal dishes, as are tomatoes, garlic and fresh herbs. For this colorful dish, sautéed scallops, cherry tomatoes and zucchini are tossed with linguine, lemony broth and fresh basil.

1 Bring a large covered pot of water to a boil over high heat. Add the pasta, return to a boil and cook for 3 to 4 minutes or according to package directions until the pasta floats to the surface and is al dente. Drain in a colander and transfer to a heated serving bowl. Toss the pasta with 2 tablespoons of the broth-water mixture and ½ teaspoon of the oil.

2 In a large, deep skillet, warm the remaining 1 tablespoon oil over high heat. Stir in the onions, bell peppers and garlic, and sauté, stirring often, for 5 minutes, or until the vegetables begin to soften.

3 Stir in the scallops, cherry tomatoes and zucchini, and sauté, tossing frequently, for 4 to 6 minutes, or until the vegetables are crisp-tender and the scallops are just cooked through. Add the remaining broth mixture, the lemon juice, black pepper and salt, and bring just to a boil, stirring. Remove the pan from the heat.

4 Pour the scallop mixture over the pasta; sprinkle with the basil and toss to mix.

Preparation time 15 minutes • **Total time** 40 minutes • **Per serving** 335 calories, 7.5 g. fat (20% of calories), 0.7 g. saturated fat, 93 mg. cholesterol, 381 mg. sodium, 2.4 g. dietary fiber, 130 mg. calcium, 4 mg. iron, 73 mg. vitamin C, 1.2 mg. beta-carotene • **Serves 4**

To ensure even cooking, halve or quarter any particularly large scallops.

FOR A CHANGE
For an even more colorful dish, use spinach or tomato pasta.

ON THE MENU
A suitably sunny dessert is perfectly ripe fruit. Choose peaches or nectarines, strawberries, raspberries or cherries.

MARKET AND PANTRY
Scallops are almost always sold shucked, so there's no guesswork involved in selecting the best: Perfectly fresh scallops smell sweet and ocean-fresh; they look plump and moist. Scallops are very perishable and should be used within a day or two of purchase.

GREEN NOODLES WITH GARLICKY SHRIMP

12 ounces medium shrimp, thawed if frozen

4 garlic cloves (1 crushed, 3 thinly sliced)

1 tablespoon extra-virgin olive oil

½ teaspoon dried oregano, crushed

¼ teaspoon freshly ground black pepper

¼ teaspoon salt

⅛–¼ teaspoon crushed red pepper flakes

8 ounces fresh spinach fettuccine or regular fettuccine

½ cup defatted chicken broth

12 ounces fresh spinach, tough stems removed, well washed

Because most seafood has rather delicate flesh, it can benefit from even very brief marinating. Allowing the shrimp to marinate in olive oil, garlic, herbs and spices for just five minutes suffuses them with an impressive jolt of flavor.

1 Bring a large covered pot of water to a boil over high heat.

2 Meanwhile, peel and devein the shrimp; leave the tails on. Place the shrimp in a medium bowl and add the crushed clove of garlic, ½ teaspoon of the olive oil, the oregano, ⅛ teaspoon of the black pepper, ⅛ teaspoon of the salt and the red pepper; toss to combine. Cover and let stand for 5 minutes.

3 While the shrimp marinates, add the pasta to the boiling water; return to a boil and cook, stirring frequently, for 3 to 4 minutes or according to package directions until the pasta floats to the surface and is tender. Drain the pasta in a colander and transfer to a serving bowl. Mix in ¼ cup of the broth to keep the pasta from sticking together.

4 Sauté the shrimp in a heavy, medium no-stick skillet over high heat for 4 to 6 minutes, or until the shrimp are pink and cooked through. Remove from the heat and set aside.

5 In the pasta cooking pot, combine the remaining 2½ teaspoons olive oil, the sliced garlic, the remaining ⅛ teaspoon salt and remaining ⅛ teaspoon black pepper; sauté, stirring constantly, for 2 to 3 minutes, or until the garlic turns light brown and is very fragrant. Slowly pour in the remaining ¼ cup broth (the broth will boil up).

6 Add the spinach, in batches, and cook for 1 to 2 minutes, or until the spinach is just wilted.

7 Spoon the spinach mixture and the shrimp over the pasta, and toss to mix.

Preparation time 25 minutes • **Total time** 45 minutes • **Per serving** 314 calories, 7.7 g. fat (22% of calories), 0.8 g. saturated fat, 204 mg. cholesterol, 490 mg. sodium, 1.6 g. dietary fiber, 152 mg. calcium, 6 mg. iron, 19 mg. vitamin C, 2.6 mg. beta-carotene • **Serves 4**

❧ ❧ ❧

LINGUINE WITH SMOKED SALMON

- 8 ounces spinach linguine or regular linguine
- ¼ cup reduced-fat sour cream
- 3 tablespoons snipped fresh dill
- 2 teaspoons distilled white vinegar
- 1½ teaspoons bottled white horseradish
- ¼ teaspoon freshly ground black pepper
- ⅛ teaspoon salt
- 1½ cups halved yellow or red pear tomatoes, plum tomatoes or cherry tomatoes
- 1 cup thinly sliced kirby or hot-house cucumber
- 3 ounces sliced smoked salmon, cut into thin strips
- ⅓ cup thinly sliced scallions

Gourmet shops and even supermarket deli counters and mail-order gourmet catalogues offer a number of choices in smoked salmon. You can go the economy route and buy what's called lox—salty brine-cured salmon—or be a bit more extravagant, since the recipe calls for only three ounces of fish. Some of the pricier choices are cold-smoked "Nova," a domestic product; imported Scottish smoked salmon (or "Scottish-style" salmon prepared on this side of the Atlantic) and alder-smoked salmon from the Pacific Northwest.

1 Bring a large covered pot of water to a boil over high heat. Add the pasta, return to a boil and cook for 9 to 11 minutes or according to package directions until al dente. Drain in a colander, cool briefly under cold running water and drain again.

2 In a salad bowl, combine the sour cream, dill, vinegar, horseradish, pepper and salt, and whisk with a fork until blended. Add the drained pasta, the tomatoes, cucumbers, salmon and scallions, and toss gently but thoroughly.

Preparation time 15 minutes • **Total time** 25 minutes • **Per serving** 284 calories, 4.1 g. fat (13% of calories), 1.4 g. saturated fat, 10 mg. cholesterol, 267 mg. sodium, 7.4 g. dietary fiber, 61 mg. calcium, 2 mg. iron, 16 mg. vitamin C, 0.3 mg. beta-carotene • **Serves 4**

FOR A CHANGE
Smoked trout could stand in for the smoked salmon, but be particularly gentle when tossing the pasta, as the trout will break apart more readily than salmon.

ON THE MENU
A crisp *ficelle*—a long, thin loaf of French bread—would be welcome with this pasta. For dessert, fill a glass bowl with well-chilled melon balls tossed with fresh mint.

Joining the ever-popular cherry tomatoes as appealing garnishes and ingredients are diminutive yellow pear tomatoes, which you may find in farmers' markets in midsummer.

INDEX

✤ ✤ ✤